AF679395

ARALING AKTIBISTA (ARAK)

(ARAK)

CONTENTS

(ARAK)

Department
General Secretariat
January 1999

The Five Golden Rays is composed of five short articles:

1. Serve the People
2. In Memory of Comrade Norman Bethune
3. The Foolish Old Man Who Removed the Mountains
4. Combat Liberalism
5. On Correcting Mistaken Ideas in the Party

These articles were written by Comrade Mao Zedong during the period when the Chinese people were advancing their National Democratic Revolution under the leadership of the Communist Party of China.

From these short articles, Comrade Mao clearly elucidated the world-view and methods of thinking and action for a revolutionary to effectively execute their revolutionary tasks. Alongside this, counterrevolutionary habits and thinking were identified, as well as methods to combat and rectify them.

Although these articles were written at a different time and place, from 1929 to 1945, and for Chinese revolutionaries waging their National Democratic Revolution, the lessons derived from these articles are like gold that will never fade and will never lose their essence over time, wherever they are applied.

In the struggle of the exploited masses against imperialism, feudalism, and other reactions, the Five Golden Rays serves as a powerful tool for anyone who wants to remold, improve in executing tasks, strengthen their organization, and advance the revolution.

As Filipino revolutionaries, we must study the spirit and objectives of these articles. The Five Golden Rays must be continually read and studied both individually and collectively. In studying these lessons, we must ensure they are lively and properly reflective of our own experiences.

The old Lesson I was included at the end of the Five Golden Rays. It is amended through the addition of explanations of certain questions and includes some questions to give more emphasis.

To other points and matters relating to revolutionary attitude, this can be used as a study guide in studying Mao's articles in the Five Golden Rays.

Serve The People

September 8, 1944

This speech was delivered by Comrade Mao Zedong at a memorial meeting for Comrade Zhang Side, held by departments directly under the Central Committee of the Communist Party.

Our Communist Party and the Eighth Route and New Fourth Armies led by our Party are battalions of the revolution. These battalions of ours are wholly dedicated to the liberation of the people and work entirely in the people's interests. Comrade Zhang Side was in the ranks of these battalions.

All people must die, but death can vary in its significance. The ancient Chinese writer Sima Qian said, "Though death befalls all people alike, it may be weightier than Mount Tai or lighter than a feather." To die for the people is weightier than Mount Tai, but to work for the fascists and die for the exploiters and oppressors is lighter than a feather. Comrade Zhang Side died for the people, and his death is indeed weightier than Mount Tai.

If we have shortcomings, we are not afraid to have them pointed out and criticized because we serve the people. Anyone, no matter who, may point out our shortcomings. If he or she is right, we will correct them. If what he or she proposes will benefit the people, we will act upon it. The idea of "better troops and simpler administration" was put forward by Mr. Li Dingming, who is not a Communist. He made a good suggestion which is of benefit to the people, and we have adopted it. If, in the interests of the people, we persist in doing what is right and correct what is wrong, our ranks will surely thrive. We hail from all corners of the country and have joined together for a common revolutionary objective. And we need the vast majority of the people with us on the road to this objective. Today, we already lead base areas with a population of 91 million, but this is not enough; to liberate the whole nation, more are needed. In times of difficulty, we must not lose sight of our achievements, must see the bright future, and must pluck up our courage. The Chinese people are suffering; it is our duty to save them, and we must exert ourselves in struggle. Wherever there is struggle, there is sacrifice, and death is a common occurrence. But we have the interests of the people and the sufferings of the great majority at heart, and when we die for the people, it is a worthy death. Nevertheless, we should do our best to avoid unnecessary sacrifices. Our cadres must show concern for every soldier, and all people in the revolutionary ranks must care for each other, must love and help each other. From now on, when anyone in our ranks who has done some useful work dies, be he soldier or cook, we should have a funeral ceremony and a memorial meeting in his honor. This should become the rule. And it should be introduced among the people as well. When someone dies in a village, let a memorial meeting be held. In this way, we express our mourning for the dead and unite all the people.

The Foolish Old Man Who Removed The Mountains

June 11, 1945

This was Comrade Mao Zedong's concluding speech at the Seventh National Congress of the Communist Party of China.

We have had a very successful congress. We have done three things. First, we have decided on the line of our Party is to boldly mobilize the masses and expand the people's forces so that, under the leadership of our Party, they will defeat the Japanese aggressors, liberate the whole people, and build a new democratic China.

Second, we have adopted the new Party Constitution.

Third, we have elected the leading body of the Party—the Central Committee. Henceforth, our task is to lead the whole membership in carrying out the Party line. Ours has been a congress of victory, a congress of unity. The delegates have made excellent comments on the three reports. Many comrades have undertaken self-criticism; with unity as the objective, unity has been achieved through self-criticism. This congress is a model of unity, self-criticism, and inner-Party democracy.

When the congress closes, many comrades will be leaving for their posts and the various war fronts. Comrades, wherever you go, you should propagate the line of the congress and, through the members of the Party, explain it to the broad masses.

Our aim in propagating the line of the congress is to build up the confidence of the whole Party and the entire people in the certain triumph of the revolution. We must first raise the political consciousness of the vanguard so that, resolute and unafraid of sacrifice, they will surmount every difficulty to win victory. But this is not enough; we must also arouse the political consciousness of the entire people so that they may willingly and gladly fight together with us for victory.

We should fire the whole people with the conviction that China belongs not to the reactionaries but to the Chinese people. There is an ancient Chinese fable called "The Foolish Old Man Who Removed the Mountains." It tells of an old man who lived in northern China long, long ago and was known as the Foolish Old Man of North Mountain. His house faced south and beyond his doorway stood the two great peaks, Taihang and Wangwu, obstructing the way. He called his sons, and hoe in hand, they began to dig up these mountains with great determination.

Another greybeard, known as the Wise Old Man, saw them and said derisively, "How silly of you to do this! It is quite impossible for you few to dig up these two huge mountains," said the Wise Old Man.

The Foolish Old Man replied, "When I die, my sons will carry on; when they die, there will be my grandsons, and then their sons and grandsons, and so on to infinity. High as they are, the mountains cannot grow any higher, and with every bit we dig, they will be that much lower. Why can't we clear them away?"

Having refuted the Wise Old Man's wrong view, he went on digging every day, unshaken in his conviction. God was moved by this, and He sent down two angels, who carried the mountains away on their backs.

Today, two big mountains lie like a dead weight on the Chinese people. One is imperialism, the other is feudalism. The Chinese Communist Party has long made up its mind to dig them up. We must persevere and work unceasingly, and we, too, will touch God's heart. Our God is none other than the masses of the Chinese people. If they stand up and dig together with us, why can't these two mountains be cleared away?

Yesterday, in a talk with two Americans who were leaving for the United States, I said that the US government was trying to undermine us and this would not be permitted. We oppose the US government's policy of supporting Chiang Kai-shek against the Communists. But we must draw a distinction, firstly, between the people of the United States and their government and, secondly, within the US government between the policymakers and their subordinates.

I said to these two Americans, "Tell the policymakers in your government that we forbid you Americans to enter the Liberated Areas because your policy is to support Chiang Kai-shek against the Communists, and we have to be on our guard. You can come to the Liberated Areas if your purpose is to fight Japan, but there must first be an agreement. We will not permit you to nose around everywhere. Since Patrick J. Hurley has publicly declared against cooperation with the Chinese

Communist Party, why do you still want to come and prowl around in our Liberated Areas?"

The US government's policy of supporting Chiang Kai-shek against the Communists shows the brazenness of the US reactionaries. But all the scheming of the reactionaries, whether Chinese or foreign, to prevent the Chinese people from achieving victory is doomed to failure. The democratic forces are the main current in the world today, while reaction is only a countercurrent. The reactionary countercurrent is trying to swamp the main current of national independence and people's democracy, but it can never become the main current.

Today, there are still three major contradictions in the old world, as Stalin pointed out long ago:

1. The contradiction between the proletariat and the bourgeoisie in the imperialist countries.
2. The contradiction between the various imperialist powers.
3. The contradiction between the colonial and semi-colonial countries and the imperialist metropolitan countries.

Not only do these three contradictions continue to exist, but they are becoming more acute and widespread. Because of their existence and growth, the time will come when the reactionary antiSoviet, anti-Communist, and anti-democratic countercurrent still in existence today will be swept away.

At this moment, two congresses are being held in

China: the Sixth National Congress of the Kuomintang and the Seventh National Congress of the Communist Party. They have completely different aims:

- The aim of the Kuomintang is to liquidate the Communist Party and all the other democratic forces in China, thus plunging China into darkness.
- The aim of the Communist Party is to overthrow Japanese imperialism and its lackeys, the Chinese feudal forces, and build a new-democratic China, thus leading China to light.

These two lines are in conflict with each other. We firmly believe that, led by the Chinese Communist Party and guided by the line of its Seventh Congress, the movement will progress towards its goals.

For more insights, see Joseph Stalin's "The Foundations of Leninism," Foreign Languages Press, Paris, 2020.

Chinese people will achieve complete victory, while the Kuomintang's counter-revolutionary line will inevitably fail.

(ARAK)

In Memory of Comrade Norman Bethune

December 21, 1939

Comrade Norman Bethune, a member of the Communist Party of Canada, was around fifty when he was sent by the Communist Parties of Canada and the United States to China. He made light of traveling thousands of miles to help us in our War of Resistance Against Japan. He arrived in Yanan in the spring of last year, went to work in the Wutai Mountains, and to our great sorrow, died a martyr at his post.

What kind of spirit is this that makes a foreigner selflessly adopt the cause of the Chinese people's liberation as his own? It is the spirit of internationalism, the spirit of communism, from which every Chinese Communist must learn. Leninism teaches that the world revolution can only succeed if the proletariat of the capitalist countries supports the struggle for liberation of the colonial and semi-colonial peoples and if the proletariat of the colonies and semi-colonies supports that of the proletariat of the capitalist countries. Comrade Bethune put this Leninist line into practice. We Chinese Communists must also follow this line in our practice.

We must unite with the proletariat of all the capitalist countries, with the proletariat of Japan, Britain, the United States, Germany, Italy, and all other capitalist countries, for this is the only way to overthrow imperialism, to liberate our nation and people, and to liberate the other nations and peoples of the world. This is our internationalism, the internationalism with which we oppose both narrow nationalism and narrow patriotism.

Comrade Bethune's spirit, his utter devotion to others without any thought of self, was shown in his great sense of responsibility in his work and his great warm-heartedness towards all comrades and the people. Every Communist must learn from him.

There are not a few people who are irresponsible in their work, preferring the light and shirking the heavy, passing the burdensome tasks on to others and choosing the easy ones for themselves. At every turn, they think of themselves before others. When they make some small contribution, they swell with pride and brag about it for fear that others will not know. They feel no warmth towards comrades and the people but are cold, indifferent, and apathetic. In truth, such people are not Communists, or at least cannot be counted as devoted Communists.

No one who returned from the front failed to express admiration for Bethune whenever his name was mentioned, and none remained unmoved by his spirit. In the Shanxi-Chahar-Hebei border area, no soldier or civilian was unmoved who had been treated by Dr. Bethune or had seen how he worked. Every Communist must learn this true communist spirit from Comrade Bethune.

Comrade Bethune was a doctor; the art of healing was his profession, and he was constantly perfecting his skill, which stood very high in the Eighth Route Army's medical service. His example is an excellent lesson for those people who wish to change their work the moment they see something different and for those who despise technical work as of no consequence or as promising no future.

Comrade Bethune and I met only once. Afterwards, he wrote me many letters. But I was busy, and I wrote him only one letter and do not even know if he ever received it. I am deeply grieved over his death. Now we are all commemorating him, which shows how profoundly his spirit inspires everyone. We must all learn the spirit of absolute selflessness from him. With this spirit, everyone can be very useful to the people. A man's ability may be great or small, but if he has this spirit, he is already noble-minded and pure, a man of moral integrity and above vulgar interests, a man who is of value to the people.

(ARAK)

Combat Liberalism

September 7, 1937

We stand for active ideological struggle because it is the weapon for ensuring unity within the Party and the revolutionary organizations in the interest of our fight. Every Communist and revolutionary should take up this weapon.

But liberalism rejects ideological struggle and stands for unprincipled peace, thus giving rise to a decadent, philistine attitude and bringing about political degeneration in certain units and individuals in the Party and the revolutionary organizations.

Liberalism manifests itself in various ways:

1. To let things slide for the sake of peace and friendship when a person has clearly gone wrong, and refrain from principled argument because he is an old acquaintance, a fellow townsman, a schoolmate, a close friend, a loved one, an old colleague, or an old subordinate. Or to touch on the matter lightly instead of going into it thoroughly, so as to keep on good terms. The result is that both the organization and the individual are harmed. This is one type of liberalism.

2. To indulge in irresponsible criticism in private instead of actively putting forward one's

suggestions to the organization. To say nothing to people to their faces but to gossip behind their backs, or to say nothing at a meeting but to gossip afterwards. To show no regard at all for the principles of collective life but to follow one's own inclination. This is a second type.

3. To let things drift if they do not affect one personally; to say as little as possible while knowing perfectly well what is wrong, to be worldly wise and play safe and seek only to avoid blame. This is a third type.
4. Not to obey orders but to give pride of place to one's own opinions. To demand special consideration from the organization but to reject its authority.

Discipline. This is a fourth type.

- To indulge in personal attacks, pick quarrels, vent personal spite, or seek revenge instead of entering into an argument and struggling against incorrect views for the sake of unity or progress or getting the work done properly. This is a fifth type.
- To hear incorrect views without rebutting them and even to hear counterrevolutionary remarks without reporting them, but instead to take them calmly as if nothing had happened. This is a sixth type.
- To be among the masses and fail to conduct propaganda and agitation or speak at meetings or conduct investigations and inquiries among them, and instead to be indifferent to them and show no concern for their well-being, forgetting that one is a

Communist and behaving as if one were an ordinary non-Communist. This is a seventh type.

- To see someone harming the interests of the masses and yet not feel indignant, or dissuade or stop him or reason with him, but to allow him to continue. This is an eighth type.
- To work half-heartedly without a definite plan or direction; to work perfunctorily and muddle along—"So long as one remains a monk, one goes on tolling the bell." This is a ninth type.
- To regard oneself as having rendered great service to the revolution, to pride oneself on being a veteran, to disdain minor assignments while being quite unequal to major tasks, to be slipshod in work and slack in study. This is a tenth type.
- To be aware of one's own mistakes and yet make no attempt to correct them, taking a liberal attitude towards oneself. This is an eleventh type.

We could name more. But these eleven are the principal types. They are all manifestations of liberalism.

Liberalism is extremely harmful in a revolutionary collective. It is a corrosive that eats away at unity, undermines cohesion, causes apathy, and creates dissension. It robs the revolutionary ranks of compact organization and strict discipline, prevents policies from being carried through, and alienates the Party organizations from the masses which the Party leads. It is an extremely bad tendency.

Liberalism stems from petit-bourgeois selfishness; it places personal interests first and the interests of the revolution second, and this gives rise to ideological, political, and organizational liberalism.

People who are liberals look upon the principles of Marxism as abstract dogma. They approve of Marxism but are not prepared to practice it or to practice it in full; they are not prepared to replace their liberalism with Marxism. These people have their Marxism, but they have their liberalism as well—they talk Marxism but practice liberalism; they apply Marxism to others but liberalism to themselves. They keep both kinds of goods in stock and find a use for each. This is how the minds of certain people work.

Liberalism is a manifestation of opportunism and conflicts fundamentally with Marxism. It is negative and objectively has the effect of helping the enemy; that is why the enemy welcomes its preservation in our midst. Such being its nature, there should be no place for it in the ranks of the revolution.

We must use Marxism, which is positive in spirit, to overcome liberalism, which is negative.

A Communist should have largeness of mind, and he should be staunch and active, looking upon the interests of the revolution as his very life and subordinating his personal interests to those of the revolution. Always and everywhere, he should adhere to principle and wage a tireless struggle against all incorrect ideas and actions so as to consolidate the collective life of the Party and strengthen the ties between the Party and the masses. He should be more concerned about the Party and the masses than about any private person, and more concerned about others than about himself. Only thus can he be considered a Communist.

All loyal, honest, active, and upright Communists must unite to oppose the liberal tendencies shown by certain people among us, and set them on the right path. This is one of the tasks on our ideological front.

On correcting mistaken ideas in the Party

December 1929

This article was a resolution drawn up by Comrade Mao Zedong for the Ninth Party Congress of the Fourth Army of the Red Army. The building of the Chinese people's armed forces was a difficult process. The Chinese Red Army (which became the Eighth Route and New Fourth Armies during the War of Resistance Against Japan and is now the People's Liberation Army) was created on August 1, 1927, during the Nanchang Uprising, and by December 1929 had been in existence for over two years.

During this period, the Communist Party organization in the Red Army learned a great deal and gained a rich store of experience in combating various mistaken ideas. The resolution summed up this experience, enabling the Red Army to build itself entirely on a Marxist-Leninist basis and eliminate all influences of armies of the old type.

This resolution was carried out not only in the Fourth Army but also in all other units of the Red Army successively. In this way, the whole Chinese Red Army became a genuine army of the people in every respect. Over the last thirty years or so, the Chinese people's armed forces have made tremendous developments and innovations in their Party activities and political work, presenting a very different picture, but the basic line remains the same as that laid down in this resolution.

There are various non-proletarian ideas in the Communist Party organization in the Fourth Red Army that greatly hinder the application of the Party's correct line. Unless these ideas are thoroughly corrected, the Fourth Army cannot possibly shoulder the tasks assigned to it in China's great revolutionary struggle. The source of such incorrect ideas in this Party Organization lies, of course, in the fact that its basic units are composed largely of peasants and other elements of petitbourgeois origin. Yet, the failure of the Party's leading bodies to wage a concerted and determined struggle against these incorrect ideas and to educate the members in the Party's correct line is also an important cause of their existence and growth.

In accordance with the spirit of the September letter of the Central Committee, this congress hereby points out the manifestations of various non-proletarian ideas in the Party organization in the Fourth Army, their sources, and the methods of correcting them, and calls upon all comrades to eliminate them thoroughly.

On the Purely Military Viewpoint

The purely military viewpoint is very highly developed among a number of comrades in the Red Army. It manifests itself as follows:

1. **Opposition of Military Affairs and Politics:** These comrades regard military affairs and politics as opposed to each other and refuse to recognize that military affairs are only one means of accomplishing political tasks. Some even say, "If you are good militarily, naturally you are good politically; if you are not good militarily, you cannot be any good politically." This is to go a step further and give military affairs a leading position over politics.
2. **Misunderstanding of the Red Army's Task:** They think that the task of the Red Army, like that of the White Army, is merely to fight. They do not understand that the Chinese Red Army is an armed body for carrying out the political tasks of the revolution. Especially at present, the Red Army should certainly not confine itself to fighting; besides fighting to destroy the enemy's military strength, it should shoulder such important tasks as doing propaganda among the masses, organizing the masses, arming them, helping them to establish revolutionary political power, and setting up Party organizations. The Red Army fights not merely for the sake of fighting but in order to conduct propaganda among the masses,

organize them, arm them, and help them to establish revolutionary political power. Without these objectives, fighting loses its meaning and the Red Army loses the reason for its existence.

3. **Organizational Subordination:** Organizationally, these comrades subordinate the departments of the Red Army doing political work to those doing military work.

Put forward the slogan, "Let Army Headquarters handle outside matters." If allowed to develop, this idea would involve the danger of estrangement from the masses, control of the government by the army, and departure from proletarian leadership— it would be to take the path of warlordism like the Kuomintang army.

1. **Propaganda Work**: They overlook the importance of propaganda teams. On the question of mass organization, they neglect the organizing of soldiers' committees in the army and the organizing of the local workers and peasants. As a result, both propaganda and organizational work are abandoned.
2. **Battle Attitude**: They become conceited when a battle is won and dispirited when a battle is lost.
3. **Selfish Departmentalism**: They think only of the Fourth Army and do not realize that it is an important task of the Red Army to arm the local masses. This is cliquism in a magnified form.
4. **Limited Vision**: Unable to see beyond their limited environment in the Fourth Army, a few comrades believe that no other revolutionary forces exist. Hence their extreme addiction to

the idea of conserving strength and avoiding action. This is a remnant of opportunism.

Some comrades, disregarding the subjective and objective conditions, suffer from the malady of revolutionary impetuosity; they will not take pains to do minute and detailed work among the masses, but riddled with illusions, want only to do big things. This is a remnant of putschism.

The sources of the purely military viewpoint are:

1. **Low Political Level**: From this flows the failure to recognize the role of political leadership in the army and to recognize that the Red Army and the White Army are fundamentally different.
2. **Mentality of Mercenaries**: Many prisoners captured in past battles have joined the Red Army, and such elements bring with them a markedly mercenary outlook, thereby providing a basis in the lower ranks for the purely military viewpoint.

For a brief period after the defeat of the revolution in 1927, a "Left" putschist tendency arose in the Communist Party. Regarding the Chinese revolution as a "permanent revolution" and the revolutionary situation in China as a "permanent upsurge," the putschist comrades refused to organize an orderly retreat and, adopting the methods of commandism and relying only on a small number of Party members.

A small section of the masses erroneously attempted to stage a series of local uprisings throughout the country, which had no prospect of success. Such putschist activities were widespread at the end of 1927 but gradually subsided in the beginning of 1928, though sentiments in favor of putschism still survived among some comrades.

From the two preceding causes, there arises a third: overconfidence in military strength and absence of confidence in the strength of the masses of the people.

The Party's failure to actively attend to and discuss military work is also a reason for the emergence of the purely military viewpoint among a number of comrades.

Methods of Correction

1. **Raise the political level in the Party through education**, destroy the theoretical roots of the purely military viewpoint, and clarify the fundamental difference between the Red Army and the White Army. At the same time, eliminate the remnants of opportunism and putschism and break down the selfish departmentalism of the Fourth Army.
2. **Intensify the political training of officers and men**, especially the education of exprisoners. Allow local governments to select workers and peasants experienced in struggle to join the Red

Army, thus organizationally weakening or even eradicating the purely military viewpoint.

3. **Arouse the local Party organizations to criticize** the Party organizations in the Red Army and the organs of mass political power to criticize the Red Army itself, to influence the Party organizations and the officers and men of the Red Army.
4. **The Party must actively attend to and discuss military work.** All the work must be discussed and decided upon by the Party before being carried out by the rank and file.
5. **Draw up Red Army rules and regulations** which clearly define its tasks, the relationship between its military and political apparatus, the relationship between the Red Army and the masses of the people, and the powers and functions of the soldiers' committees and their relationship with the military and political organizations.

(ARAK)

On Ultra-Democracy

Since the Fourth Army of the Red Army accepted the directives of the Central Committee, there has been a great decrease in the manifestations of ultrademocracy. For example, Party decisions are now carried out fairly well, and no longer does anyone bring up such erroneous demands as that the Red Army should apply "democratic centralism from the bottom to the top" or should "let the lower levels discuss all problems first, and then let the higher levels decide."

Actually, however, this decrease is only temporary and superficial and does not mean that ultrademocratic ideas have already been eliminated. In other words, ultra-democracy is still deep-rooted in the minds of many comrades. Witness the various expressions of reluctance to carry out Party decisions.

The methods of correction are as follows:

1. **In the sphere of theory, destroy the roots of ultra-democracy.** First, it should be pointed out that the danger of ultra-democracy lies in the fact that it damages or even completely wrecks the Party organization and weakens or even completely undermines the Party's fighting capacity, rendering the Party incapable of fulfilling its fighting tasks and thereby causing the defeat of the revolution. Next, it should be pointed out that the source of ultra-democracy consists in the petit-bourgeoisie's individualistic

aversion to discipline. When this characteristic is brought into the Party, it develops into ultrademocratic ideas politically and organizationally. These ideas are utterly incompatible with the fighting tasks of the proletariat.

2. **In the sphere of organization, ensure democracy under centralized guidance.** It should be done on the following lines:

(a) The leading bodies of the Party must give a correct line of guidance and find solutions when problems arise, in order to establish themselves as centers of leadership.

(b) The higher bodies must be familiar with the life of the masses and with the situation in the lower bodies so as to have an objective basis for correct guidance.

(c) No Party organization at any level should make casual decisions in solving problems. Once a decision is reached, it must be firmly carried out.

(d) All decisions of any importance made by the Party's higher bodies must be promptly transmitted to the lower bodies and the Party rank and file. The method is to call meetings of activists or general membership meetings of the Party branches or even of the columns (when circumstances permit) and to assign people to make reports at such meetings.

On Disregard of Organizational Discipline

Disregard of organizational discipline in the Party organization in the Fourth Army manifests itself as follows:

A. Failure of the minority to submit to the majority

For example, when a minority finds its motion voted down, it does not sincerely carry out the Party decisions.

The methods of correction are as follows:

1. At meetings, all participants should be encouraged to voice their opinions as fully as possible. The rights and wrongs in any controversy should be clarified without compromise or glossing over. In order to reach a clear-cut conclusion, what cannot be settled at one meeting should be discussed at another, provided there is no interference with the work.
2. One requirement of Party discipline is that the minority should submit to the majority. If the view of the minority has been rejected, it must support the decision passed by the majority. If necessary, it can bring up the matter for reconsideration at the next meeting, but apart from that, it must not act against the decision in any way.

B. Criticism made without regard to organizational discipline

1. Inner-Party criticism is a weapon for strengthening the Party organization and increasing its fighting capacity. In the Party organization of the Red Army, however, criticism is not always of this character, and sometimes turns into personal attack. As a result, it damages the Party organization as well as individuals. This is a manifestation of petit-bourgeois individualism. The method of correction is to help Party members understand that the purpose of criticism is to increase the Party's fighting capacity in order to achieve victory in the class struggle and that it should not be used as a means of personal attack.
2. Many Party members make their criticisms not inside, but outside, the Party. The reason is that the general membership has not yet grasped the importance of the Party organization (its meetings and so forth) and sees no difference between criticism inside and outside the organization. The method of correction is to educate Party members so that they understand the importance of Party organization and make their criticisms of Party committees or comrades at Party meetings.

On Absolute Equalitarianism

Absolute equalitarianism became quite serious in the Red Army at one time. Here are some examples:

- On the matter of allowances to wounded soldiers, there were objections to differentiating between light and serious cases, and the demand was raised for equal allowances for all.
- When officers rode on horseback, it was regarded not as something necessary for performing their duties but as a sign of inequality.
- Absolutely equal distribution of supplies was demanded, with objections to larger allotments in special cases.
- In the hauling of rice, the demand was made that all should carry the same load on their backs, irrespective of age or physical condition.
- Equality was demanded in the allotment of billets, and the Headquarters would be abused for occupying larger rooms.
- Equality was demanded in the assignment of fatigue duties, and there was unwillingness to do a little more than the next man.
- It even went so far that when there were two wounded men but only one stretcher, neither could be carried away because each refused to yield priority to the other.

Absolute equalitarianism, as shown in these examples, is still very serious among officers and soldiers of the Red

Army. Like ultra-democracy in political matters, it is the product of a handicraft and small peasant economy—the only difference being that one manifests itself in material affairs, while the other manifests itself in political affairs.

The Method of Correction

We should point out that, before the abolition of capitalism, absolute equalitarianism is a mere illusion of peasants and small proprietors. Even under socialism, there can be no absolute equality, for material things will then be distributed on the principle of "from each according to his ability, to each according to his work" as well as on that of meeting the needs of the work.

The distribution of material things in the Red Army must be more or less equal, as in the case of equal pay for officers and men, because this is required by the present circumstances of the struggle. But absolute equalitarianism beyond reason must be opposed because it is not required by the struggle; on the contrary, it hinders the struggle.

On Subjectivism

Subjectivism exists to a serious degree among some Party members, causing great harm to the analysis of the political situation and the guidance of the work. The reason is that subjective analysis of a political situation and subjective guidance of work inevitably result either in opportunism or in putschism. As for subjective criticism, loose and groundless talk or suspiciousness, such practices inside the Party often breed unprincipled disputes and undermine the Party organization.

Another point that should be mentioned in connection with inner Party criticism is that some comrades ignore the major issues and confine their attention to minor points when they make their criticism. They do not understand that the main task of criticism is to point out political and organizational mistakes. As to personal shortcomings, unless they are related to political and organizational mistakes, there is no need to be over-critical and to embarrass the comrades concerned. Moreover, once such criticism develops, there is the great danger that the Party members will concentrate entirely on minor faults, and everyone will become timid and overcautious and forget the Party's political tasks.

The main method of correction is to educate Party members so that a political and scientific spirit pervades their thinking and their Party life. To this end, we must:

1. **Teach Party members** to apply the MarxistLeninist method in analyzing a political

situation and appraising the class forces, instead of making a subjective analysis and appraisal.

2. **Direct the attention of Party members** to social and economic investigation and study, so as to determine the tactics of struggle and methods of work, and help comrades to understand that without investigation of actual conditions they will fall into the pit of fantasy and putschism.

3. In inner-Party criticism, **guard against subjectivism, arbitrariness, and the vulgarization of criticism**; statements should be based on facts and criticism should center on politics.

On Individualism

The tendency towards individualism in the Red Army Party organization manifests itself as follows:

1. **Retaliation**

   Some comrades, after being criticized inside the Party by a soldier comrade, look for opportunities to retaliate outside the Party, often by beating or abusing the comrade in question. They also seek to retaliate within the Party: "You have criticized me at this meeting, so I'll find some way to pay you back at the next." Such retaliation arises from purely personal considerations, neglecting the interests of the class and the Party as a whole. Its target is not the enemy class, but individuals in our own ranks, acting as a corrosive that weakens the organization and its fighting capacity.

2. **"Small group" mentality**

   Some comrades consider only the interests of their own small group and ignore the general interest. Although on the surface this does not seem to be the pursuit of personal interests, it exemplifies the narrowest individualism and has a strong corrosive and centrifugal effect. "Small group" mentality used to be rife in the Red Army, and although there has been some improvement as a result of criticism, there are still survivals, and further effort is needed to overcome it.

3. **The "employee" mentality**

   Some comrades do not understand that the Party and the Red Army, of which they are members, are both instruments for carrying out the tasks of the revolution. They do not realize that they themselves are makers of the revolution, but think that their responsibility is merely to their individual superiors and not to the revolution. This passive mentality of an "employee" of the revolution is also a manifestation of individualism. It explains why there are not very many activists who work unconditionally for the revolution. Unless it is eliminated, the number of activists will not grow, and the heavy burden of the revolution will remain on the shoulders of a small number of people, much to the detriment of the struggle.

4. **Pleasure-seeking**
   In the Red Army, there are also quite a few people whose individualism finds expression in pleasure-seeking. They always hope that their unit will march into big cities. They want to go there not to work but to enjoy themselves. The last thing they want is to work in the Red areas where life is hard.
5. **Passivity**
   Some comrades become passive and stop working whenever anything goes against them and their wishes. This is mainly due to lack of education, though sometimes it is also due to the leadership's improper conduct of affairs, assignment of work, or enforcement of discipline.
6. **The Desire to Leave the Army**

- The number of people who ask for transfers from the Red Army to local work is on the increase. The reason for this does not lie entirely with the individuals but also with:
- The material hardships of life in the Red Army
- Exhaustion after a long struggle
- The leadership's improper conduct of affairs, assignment of work, or enforcement of discipline
- The method of correction is primarily to strengthen education so as to rectify individualism ideologically. Next, it is to conduct

affairs, make assignments, and enforce discipline in a proper way. In addition, ways must be found to improve the material life of the Red Army, and every available opportunity must be utilized for rest and rehabilitation in order to improve material conditions. In our educational work, we must explain that in its social origin, individualism is a reflection within the Party of petit-bourgeois and bourgeois ideas.

On the Ideology of Roving Rebel Bands

The political ideology of roving rebel bands has emerged in the Red Army because the proportion of vagabond elements is large and because there are great masses of vagabonds in China, especially in the southern provinces. This ideology manifests itself as follows:

o Some people want to increase our political influence only by means of roving guerrilla actions but are unwilling to increase it by undertaking the arduous task of building up base areas and establishing the people's political power.

o In expanding the Red Army, some people follow the line of "hiring men and buying horses" and "recruiting deserters and accepting mutineers," rather than the line of expanding the local Red Guards and the local troops and thus developing the main forces of the Red Army. o

Some people lack the patience to carry on arduous struggles together with the masses and only want to go to the big cities to eat and drink to their hearts' content.

All these manifestations of the ideology of roving rebels seriously hamper the Red Army in performing its proper tasks; consequently, its eradication is an important objective in the ideological struggle within the Red Army Party organization. It must be understood that the ways of roving rebels of the Huang Chao or these two Chinese idioms refer to the methods which some rebels in Chinese history adopted to expand their forces. In the application of these methods, attention was paid to numbers rather than to quality, and people of all sorts were indiscriminately recruited to swell the ranks.

Huang Chao was the leader of the peasant revolts towards the end of the Tang Dynasty. In A.D. 875, starting from his home district Caozhou (now Heze County in Shandong), Huang led armed peasants in victorious battles against the imperial forces and styled himself the "Heaven-Storming General." In the course of a decade, he swept over most of the provinces in the Yellow, Yangtse, Huai, and Pearl river valleys, reaching as far as Guangxi.

He finally broke through the Tongguan Pass, captured the imperial capital of Changan (now Xian in Shanxi), and was crowned Emperor of Chi. Internal dissensions and attacks by the non-Han tribal allies of the Tang forces compelled Huang to abandon Changan and retreat to his native district, where he committed suicide. The ten years' war fought by him is one of the most famous peasant wars in Chinese history. Dynastic historians record that "all people suffering from heavy taxes and levies rallied to him." But as he merely carried on roving warfare without ever establishing relatively consolidated base areas, his forces were called "roving rebel bands."

(ARAK)

Correction Methods

1. **Intensify Education**: Criticize incorrect ideas and eradicate the ideology of roving rebel bands.
2. **Focused Education**: Intensify education among the basic sections of the Red Army and among recently recruited captives to counter the vagabond outlook.

3. **Recruitment Strategy**: Draw active workers and peasants experienced in struggle into the ranks of the Red Army.

Li Zhuang type are not permissible under present day conditions.

Li Zicheng, born in Shaanxi, was the leader of a peasant revolt that led to the overthrow of the Ming Dynasty. The revolt first started in northern
Shaanxi in 1628. Li joined the forces led by Gao Yingxiang, also known as King Zhuang (the Daring King), and campaigned through Henan and Anhui and back to Shaanxi. After Gao's death in 1636, Li succeeded him, becoming King Chuang, and campaigned in and out of the provinces of Shaanxi, Sichuan, Henan, and Hubei.

Finally, he captured the imperial capital of Beijing in 1644, whereupon the last Ming emperor committed suicide. The chief slogan he spread among the masses was "Support King Chuang, and pay no grain taxes." Another slogan of his to enforce discipline among his men ran: "Any murder means the killing of my father; any rape means the violation of my mother." Thus, he won the support of the masses, and his movement became the main current of the peasant revolts raging all over the country. As he, too, roamed about without ever establishing relatively consolidated base areas, he was eventually defeated by Wu Sangui, a Ming general, who colluded with the Ching troops in a joint attack on Li.

The Party organization in the Red Army has already waged struggles against putschism, but not yet to a sufficient extent. Therefore, remnants of this ideology still exist in the Red Army. Their manifestations are:

1. Blind action regardless of subjective and objective conditions
2. Inadequate and irresolute application of the Party's policies for the cities
3. Slack military discipline, especially in moments of defeat
4. Acts of house-burning by some units
5. Practices of shooting deserters and inflicting corporal punishment, both of which smack of putschism

In its social origins, putschism is a combination of lumpen-proletarian and petit-bourgeois ideology.

The methods of correction are as follows:

1. Eradicate putschism ideologically.
2. Correct putschist behavior through rules, regulations, and policies.

3. Why is the question, "For whom?" the most important and key issue every revolutionary faces?

We come from different corners of the city and the countryside, united for a single revolutionary cause. But what is our cause? It is none other than to liberate the people from imperialism, feudalism, and bureaucratic capitalism. Each of us is aware of the concrete conditions of the Filipino people. We have joined a revolutionary organization and are participating in the revolutionary movement to contribute to the achievement of the people's struggle for national liberation and democracy.

The question "For whom?" is a matter of basic revolutionary standpoint. Are we for the broad masses, the more than seventy million Filipinos who are exploited and oppressed? Or are we for the few foreign imperialists, local comprador bourgeois, and landlords who exploit and oppress? If we clearly answer the question "For whom?" all endeavors, thinking, and work can focus on serving the people and the overall effort to weaken and destroy the enemy.

As revolutionaries, our thoughts, feelings, and actions are fully focused on achieving genuine freedom for our nation and democracy for the broad masses of the Filipino people. In every moment and every action, the revolutionary's response to the question "For whom?" is only one: for the oppressed and exploited masses. This is the core of the revolutionary standpoint.

(ARAK)

Why must one be always considerate about the interests and welfare of the people and commit wholehearted service to them?

We can wholeheartedly serve the people if we always consider their welfare ahead of our own and keep the suffering of the overwhelming majority in our hearts while nurturing deep contempt against the people's enemies. We must always strive to ensure that the basic standpoint on issues and actions is to advance the interests of the people and weaken the enemy at all times. We must be diligent in learning the problems and conditions of the masses and firmly linking and uniting with them to raise their consciousness and advance:

- The building of their power and organization
- The victory of their struggles

Wholehearted service to the people also means eradicating individualism and narrow-mindedness, and prioritizing the general interests or interests of the majority. Whenever individualism prevails, a person prioritizes benefiting oneself or a small group, setting aside or subordinating the interest of the majority. Individualism not only serves one's own ego but also the interests of the reactionaries.

Maintain and benefit from the exploitative and oppressive system.

Why must every revolutionary cultivate the attitude of ceaseless and all-out effort in pushing the correct line of the People's Democratic Revolution?

The masses carry the massive burden of imperialism, feudalism, and bureaucrat capitalism. The ruling class is doing everything they can to stay in power in order to keep their status as exploiters and oppressors of the people intact. Only through revolution can the broad masses of the people free themselves from the three basic problems.

History proves that the masses are the genuine heroes. Revolution is no less than a hugely violent and decisive action of the masses to overthrow the rule of the exploitative and oppressive classes in order to establish the power of the people. No revolution has ever occurred where the masses aren't the main motive forces in dismantling the ruling class. The strength and wisdom of the masses are the core foundation for building the new society. They genuinely make history.

We must arouse the masses and raise their political consciousness. We must explain to the masses that the three basic problems are the real root of their suffering and that their liberation can only be achieved through united action. We must patiently explain to them the line of the People's Democratic Revolution so that it continually garners increasing people's support. Thus, it cannot be easily crushed nor defeated by the reactionaries.

With the effort of propagating this line and in strengthening the confidence of the people in its correctness, we are certain of the victory of the revolution. This is the way by which we awaken and unite the masses to our side, for them to participate in and give all they can to the liberation of the people from the three basic problems.

No matter how large and strong the enemy is, they will assuredly be overpowered by the unity of the people. We must relentlessly unite and build up the strength of the Peoples' Democratic Revolution
until victory. This is the key message in the article, "The Foolish Old Man Who Removed the Mountains."

Why do we need to conduct self-remolding as revolutionaries?

As revolutionaries, we have a duty to focus our minds, emotions, and actions on the basic interests of the Filipino people. However, we all still possess ideas, habits, and practices widespread in the current rotten society. We grew up in a society dominated by oppressors and exploiters. Until now, we are continually influenced by the rotten ideas of the current society. Thus, it is every revolutionary's duty to conduct self-remolding.

We change ourselves through active revolutionary work and conscious struggle against our wrong ideas, habits, and behavior. By continuing to do revolutionary tasks and always being cautious of our own weaknesses and mistakes, we can mold ourselves in the midst of the storm of struggle against the enemies of the Filipino people. We shall become stronger, overcome our weaknesses, and become more correct and more efficient in advancing the revolution.

Self-remolding cannot be accomplished in just a few hours or several days. This is a long and complex struggle. A continuous struggle and rejection of the remaining influences of the rotten system is needed. Thus, we become more correct and efficient in revolutionary work, and we can steel our determination to strive for the struggle to advance the peoples' democratic revolution until victory.

We conduct self-remolding so we can cultivate the fundamental revolutionary attitude to further effectively serve the masses and fruitfully contribute to the revolution. Every revolutionary should:

- Wholeheartedly serve the masses and always strive to be close to the masses.
- Always be ready and have no fear of sacrifice and death.
- Be serious, rigorous, and diligent in studying and performing duties.
- Always strive for unity and warmth with fellow revolutionaries.

- Be open to receiving criticisms and be ready to rectify weaknesses and mistakes.
- Be internationalist.

How do revolutionaries value duties and tasks for the revolution?

Revolutionaries value their tasks and duties and the revolution to the fullest. They know that revolutionary tasks and duties are part of the great mission to liberate the people from the clutches of exploitation and oppression. The revolutionaries value their tasks and duties by upholding the revolutionary interest of the Filipino people.

Signs that revolutionaries value their tasks and duties to the fullest:

- They are serious and diligent in attending to their work.
- They are always enthusiastic and eager to take action.
- They are always ready to accept any task necessary for the advancement of the revolution.

The revolutionaries are serious in their work. For them, their main priority is always attending to revolutionary activities and duties.

They are neat and orderly in their work, not prone to careless and reckless action. They study and look for ways to solve problems and perform work in the best way.

The revolutionaries are enthusiastic and energetic in their actions. They are forward-thinking; every movement and every step forward is a contribution to the bright future. They never feel demoralized, depressed, or lose confidence in the midst of facing problems and difficulties in the struggle. They always maintain a highly militant fighting spirit and jump to take advantage of any opportunity to advance the struggle.

The revolutionary has the mark of initiative. They are full of initiative, not only in the performance of their own tasks and duties but also in any other problem that they see and are capable of handling too.

The revolutionaries are always ready to fulfill their tasks and duties. They accept every task directed to them without measuring the value or the difficulty and sacrifice necessary to fulfill them. They do not pick and choose the work because they do not seek fame or convenience for themselves.

What is the correct view of hardship, sacrifice, and death?

The revolutionary has recognition that hardship, sacrifice, and death are an inevitable part of the liberation of the people. It is a natural part of the violent struggle between the people and the ruling classes. It is also a natural part of the revolution to overthrow the dominance of US imperialism, feudalism, and bureaucrat capitalism. They are not only natural; they are necessary in order to fight for and protect the interests of the people and the revolution. These are needed in order to wipe out oppression and exploitation, and to establish a genuine free democratic society.

The revolutionary is always ready to face hardship, make sacrifices, and even death for the sake of struggle. The revolutionary's sacrifice is significant because it is for the success of the revolution. They know that sooner or later the long-awaited and long-hoped freedom shall be seen on the horizon. In the midst of danger and crisis, the revolutionary's readiness to make sacrifices and face death provides the strength and courage to protect the interests of the people and the revolution.

In times of difficulties and crisis, the revolutionary never forgets the bright future aimed for in the struggle and for which hardships and sacrifices are made. Any crisis and hardship must never hamper the perspective nor weaken the confidence.

Revolutionaries are courageous, but they avoid unnecessary sacrifice. They don't just jump into the face of danger for the simple reason that they are steps towards genuine freedom and democracy for the people.

Are ready and willing to die. They value and take care of the safety and well-being of the masses, fellow revolutionaries, and themselves.

Why is the death of someone serving the people heavier than a mountain and the death of those serving the enemy lighter than a feather?

The death of a revolutionary is a weighty death. A revolutionary can die in several ways—in combat, from a disease or sickness, an accident, or old age. But it's not the manner of death that is decisive in the character of their death. More than anything, the weight of his or her death is measured by his or her whole-hearted dedication to the people, their tireless efforts to serve the masses and advance the revolution.

On the other hand, the death of someone serving the enemy has no honor: it is lighter than a feather. Because their life is dedicated to the exploiters and the oppressors, they have killed their humanity and thrown away their honor. For the exploited and oppressed masses, any death in the service of the enemy is looked down upon.

What is the correct attitude towards victories?

In the face of victories, it is important to guard against pride and arrogance. Always remain humble and never become intoxicated in victory. Always keep in mind the long road ahead and avoid complacency, rushing, or leniency.

What is the correct view of the masses?

The masses are the foundation for achieving any revolutionary goal. It is with their inherent intelligence and strength that a society advances and progresses. The masses are the well of undefeatable power against any foe or force hindering change. To achieve freedom, democracy, and progress, it is a must to rely on and trust the masses.

The revolutionary acknowledges and carries a great accountability and responsibility to the masses. It is their duty to uphold the interest of the masses, to foster firm unity with the masses, and to encourage them towards revolutionary change.

The revolutionary upholds the national and democratic aspirations of the masses through their diligent and responsible integration amongst the masses and their participation in their struggles.

They are patient in explaining and raising the consciousness of the masses. They are tireless in helping the masses to organize and take action to solve their problems and to fight their enemies. The revolutionary is well-known as a genuine servant of and one with the masses. They pay attention even to the small day-to-day needs and problems of the masses.

In consistently upholding the national and democratic interest of the masses, the revolutionary builds the strong and unbreakable unity between the revolutionaries who are serving and the masses who are being served. The revolutionary values and gives utmost significance to this unity. They always strive to unite with and be close to the masses. They use all the opportunities to be amongst the masses, to work and learn from them. They strictly avoid anything that violates the interest of the masses or any abuse of their kindness because such hinders the unity between the revolution and the masses.

How do revolutionaries treat fellow revolutionaries?

A revolutionary is always seeking unity with their fellow revolutionaries. They are loving and thoughtful towards their comrades. Unity with and thoughtful treatment of revolutionaries is important in building and strengthening the unity and strength of the revolutionary ranks. Revolutionaries have outstanding practice in uniting and teaching each other.

A revolutionary always unites with her or his comrades, even if they don't know each other very well, or those whom they don't share the same opinions, or those who have made errors but are willing to rectify. Insignificant misunderstandings can easily be set aside or can be overcome because the revolutionary always gives importance to unity. Their understanding of the conditions of their comrades and their effort to work and become a better revolutionary is always a priority.

A revolutionary is thoughtful and loving towards their comrades. They always help every comrade to fulfill their duties and tasks, and in resolving their problems, including personal ones. They help and give support to their comrades to forge themselves in the midst of the struggle. The joys and struggles of their comrades are also the joys and struggles of every revolutionary.

What is the correct view towards criticism and self-criticism?

Weaknesses and shortcomings are a common occurrence in the flow of a revolutionary. Oftentimes, they are results of lack of experience or are products of the wrong mindset and undesirable traits still left within us. However, the revolutionary is always ready to overcome them in order to further firmly uphold the National Democratic interests of the people.

The revolutionary is always ready to criticize their own weaknesses and mistakes. They are open to criticisms, and whatever is correct and what is good for the people is always placed above everything else. They don't refuse, nor do they doubt the need to rectify their weaknesses and mistakes. They are always ready to remold themselves in order to continue serving the people.

Criticism and Self-Criticism

Criticism and self-criticism is an effective process needed to correct mistakes and overcome weaknesses. It is essential to further strengthen unity within the revolutionary ranks and between revolutionaries and the masses. Through criticism, weaknesses and mistakes can be identified and rooted out. In this way, we learn from our mistakes to avoid them in the future.

Criticisms must always be comradely and in accordance with the spirit of "cure the sickness to save the patient." Criticism should not be made into an occasion for personal attacks or revenge. Criticisms should focus on the most important ideological, political, and organizational matters only.

Criticism and self-criticism must be conducted regularly. It ensures that our work is always analyzed, continues to improve, maintains and further strengthens our unity, and keeps us united and close to the masses.

What is internationalism?

At the current stage of imperialism, the people of various nations around the world are suffering from unabated oppression and exploitation at the hands of the imperialists. It is very important, therefore, for the unity and cooperation of the peoples of different countries to struggle against imperialism and all reactions. This is internationalism.

It is our task as Filipino revolutionaries to liberate our country from US imperialism, feudalism, and bureaucrat capitalism. The advancement of the Filipino revolution, especially its victory, helps to weaken imperialism around the world; thus, it contributes to the advancement of the struggle of the people in other countries. At the same time, people of other countries who also struggle against imperialism and other reactions also help us.

Revolutionaries always think of fulfilling their revolutionary work, not only for their own country but also for the billions of masses exploited all over the world. Through this perspective, patriotism and nationalism—love for one's own country—is correctly linked to internationalism. It is different from narrow patriotism or narrow nationalism, where they only give importance to their own country.

The interest of their own country and only see other countries and other people from the point of view of self-benefit and advantage.

It is our internationalist duty to advance the twostage Philippine revolution. The destruction of US imperialist power and local ruling classes in the Philippines shall be our biggest contribution to the dismantling of the reign of imperialism and other oppressive and exploiting classes around the world.

Our internationalist duty doesn't end with the victory of our democratic revolution. Upon the seizure of political power, it is our internationalist duty to consolidate it, establish a democratic people's state, and launch a socialist revolution. We also need to strengthen unity with the people of other countries and continue to cooperate with revolutionary and anti-imperialist movements and organizations in other nations.

Discussion Questions

1. **What are the wrong thinking and attitudes that harm the interest of the revolution and the masses? How can they be changed?**

   For this part, read and discuss all the parts of the article "Combat Liberalism" and "On Correcting Mistaken Ideas in the Party."

   a. **What is liberalism and why should we**

   combat it?

   Liberalism is the rejection or avoidance of active ideological struggle. It rejects and avoids the clarification of what are correct revolutionary ideas, policies, and actions, and which ones are incorrect and nonrevolutionary: rejection or avoidance to uphold what is correct and repudiate the wrong.

> We must combat liberalism because it is incorrect and it destroys the principled unity of the revolutionary ranks. Instead, it upholds unprincipled peace, the existence, and propagation of incorrect and nonrevolutionary ideas, policies, and actions.

Overall, the unity within the ranks of the revolutionaries is firm, particularly concerning the basic principles of the revolution. However, at various instances, especially if related to particular policies and day-to-day activity, the wrong ideas and actions crop up. It is only a reflection of the existence of struggle in lines, of correct and incorrect, and having limitations and weaknesses among the revolutionary ranks.

Every revolutionary must guard against such weaknesses and errors. Every revolutionary has a duty to always uphold and strive for what is correct, struggle against wrong ideas, and criticize to rectify the wrong actions. This is what we call active "ideological struggle." Only through this manner can we raise and strengthen the principled unity within our ranks.

What are the types of liberalism?

Liberalism manifests through the following thinking and habits:

1. **Letting wrong things slide**: Refraining from principled argument because the comrade is a close friend or touching on the matter lightly instead of going into it thoroughly, so as to keep on good terms.
2. **Irresponsible criticism**: Indulging in irresponsible criticism in private instead of actively putting forward one's suggestions to the organization; saying nothing to people's faces but gossiping behind their backs, or saying nothing at a meeting but gossiping afterward; showing no regard at all for the principles of collective life but following one's own inclination.
3. **Letting things drift**: Letting things drift if they do not affect one personally; saying as little as possible while knowing perfectly well what is wrong, being worldly wise, playing safe, and seeking only to avoid blame.

4. **Disobedience**: Disobeying orders but giving pride of place to one's own opinions; demanding special consideration from the organization but rejecting its discipline.
5. **Personal attacks**: Indulging in personal attacks, picking quarrels, venting personal spite, or seeking revenge instead of entering into an argument and struggling against incorrect views for the sake of unity or progress or getting the work done properly.

6. **Ignoring incorrect views**: Hearing incorrect views without rebutting them and even hearing counter-revolutionary remarks without reporting them, but instead taking them in calmly as if nothing had happened.
7. **Failure to engage**: Being among the masses and failing to conduct propaganda and agitation or speak at meetings or conduct investigations and inquiries; being indifferent to their well-being and showing no concern for them, forgetting that one is a Communist and behaving as if one were an ordinary non-Communist.
8. **Indifference to harm**: Seeing someone harming the interests of the masses and yet not feeling indignant, or dissuading or stopping them or reasoning with them, but allowing them to continue.
9. **Half-hearted work**: Working half-heartedly without a definite plan or direction; to work perfunctorily and muddle along—"So long as one remains a monk, one goes on tolling the bell."

x. **Regarding oneself as having rendered great service to the revolution:** • Pride in being a veteran

- Disdain for minor assignments while being unequal to major tasks
- Slipshod in work and slack in study

Being aware of one's own mistakes:

- Making no attempt to correct them
- Taking a liberal attitude towards oneself

How do you combat liberalism?

Liberalism, like rust, must be scraped to the core. Similar to a bad weed, it can only be combated by pulling it out by the roots.

Liberalism is rooted in selfishness, placing oneself above the welfare of the revolution and the interest of the majority. It is the root of rejecting active ideological struggle. This rejection stems from the desire to maintain peace, even if it is not principled. Usually, this desire is not just to avoid hurting others, but to avoid hurting self-interest: "I will not criticize you, so don't bother me."

To thoroughly combat liberalism:

- Selfishness must be rejected
- The interest of the revolution or the majority of exploited and oppressed masses must be upheld
- Stand for revolutionary principles and actively fight against all wrong ideas, actions, and tendencies
- Every revolutionary must cultivate and uphold the spirit of selflessness
- Broaden the mind to see and embrace the broader interest of the people, not just self-interest

By doing this, there is no doubt nor second thought in pursuing ideological struggle, and the strongest and most principled unity will be built.

What is the purely militarist viewpoint, where is it coming from, and how can it be corrected?

The purely militarist viewpoint involves the separation and clashing of politics and military. It refuses to subordinate military work and other issues as part of political work, viewing the people's army solely as a fighting force. This perspective neglects other tasks such as propaganda, mass work, and production, which are essential for the revolution. It fails to realize that the people's army is the primary instrument in achieving the political goals and objectives of the revolution.

This viewpoint arises from:

- A lack of understanding and appreciation of political leadership over the people's army

- A lack of understanding that the people's army is fundamentally different from the reactionary army, primarily based on the politics it serves and upholds.

Therefore, a purely militarist viewpoint can only be corrected through:

- Raising ideological and political awareness
- Conducting criticism and self-criticism
- Discussion of military issues that show the correct relationship to politics

What is ultra-democracy and violation of organizational discipline, and how can it be corrected?

Ultra-democracy is giving too much importance or insistence on democracy without the guiding principles of the organization. It means there is no consideration, or there is hesitation if not outright violation, of the principles, policies, rules, or decisions of the organization. Examples of ultrademocratic thinking include:

- "Democratic centralism from the bottom to the top"
- "All matters must be discussed first from the lower units before the higher units can make a decision"

Violation of organizational discipline can be seen from the following:

1. **The minority's refusal to follow the majority:** Not following the majority can also be seen through the lack of seriousness in implementing the decisions, if not outright refusal to implement.
2. **Giving criticisms without giving consideration to organizational discipline:** This comes in the form of personal or unprincipled criticisms or attacks, or such criticisms or attacks are made outside of meetings or outside of the organization.

Ultra-democracy destroys unity and weakens the organization. It is deeply rooted in petit-bourgeois selfishness or individualism and rejection of discipline. Additionally, if the leadership is weak and organizational discipline is loose, it creates the condition for ultra-democracy and violation of discipline to exist.

To correct this, the petit-bourgeois selfishness or individualism and rejection of organizational discipline must be uprooted. This can be done through education and active ideological struggle. The spirit of selflessness and subordinating self-interest to the interest of the whole must be upheld. The importance of the organization and the discipline within must be clear to the membership. It is also important to clarify how centralism is guided by democracy within the organization and how centralism is based on democracy.

In the organizational field, it is important to make the leadership very efficient and strengthen democratic centralism. The leadership must always ensure that they have a strong relationship with the lower units and the membership of the organization, that their ideas are considered, and that there is an effective flow of communication between them. At any level, every decision should be a result of thorough thinking and thorough discussion.

What is individualism and how can it be corrected?

Individualism

Individualism is completely taking care of one's own welfare while the welfare of the organization and the revolution are either made subordinate or set aside. Other than ultra-democracy and violation of organizational discipline, individualist tendencies can also be exemplified through the following forms:

- **Revenge**
- **Small group mentality**
- **Employee mentality**
- **Seeking pleasure**
- **Passivity or lack of enthusiasm**
- **Desire to "take a break"**
- **Separate kingdoms**

Because individualism mirrors the petit-bourgeois and bourgeois thinking inside the revolutionary movement, ideological education is the primary measure for correctness. Every single member must identify non-proletarian ideas and habits in implementing revolutionary tasks as well as for the interest of the broad masses and the people. Alongside, it is also important to conduct discussion, tasking, and the implementation of discipline according to the correct procedure to ensure the efficient response to the needs of the forces.

Absolute Egalitarianism/Absolute Equality

The thinking in absolute egalitarianism is the refusal to recognize that different individuals and units inside the organization have different conditions, capabilities, and needs. It asserts the absolute equality of everyone at all times—in setting tasks, in the disposition of comrades, and in allocating resources. It does not correspond to concrete conditions, capabilities, and needs, and prevents the forging of unity and the advancement of the revolution.

Although at first glance it appears that equality is desired, the hidden motive of absolute egalitarians is the selfish apprehension that they may be shortchanged by others. For as long as capitalism is not vanquished and the bourgeoisie is not completely defeated, absolute egalitarianism remains the illusion of peasants and small proprietors.

To correct this kind of thinking, it must be clarified to the revolutionary ranks that the distribution of material needs and tasks is primarily set by the concrete needs in the struggle. In the ideological field, it is important to clarify that it is impossible to have absolute equality. This is true not only under the capitalist and semi-feudal system but even under socialism.

Subjectivism

Subjectivism is the outlook of looking at things one-sidedly, not based on concrete reality but on wrong supposition. Subjectivism is is already forming conclusions even with a lack of investigation.. Subjectivism is having a wrong analysis and forming incorrect conclusions, often due to a lack of investigation. This results in wrong policies and decisions. An example is giving undue importance to certain personal weaknesses without properly contextualizing them or connecting them to political and organizational work.

Subjectivism is rooted in a non-scientific and nonproletarian outlook and ways of thinking. It harms the organization by resulting in wrong policies and decisions and leads to unprincipled struggles that weaken the organization.

To combat subjectivism, it is necessary to promote and uphold the proletarian scientific outlook and method while repudiating bourgeois and petit bourgeois outlooks and ways of thinking. Diligent study is necessary in conducting investigations and analysis, particularly social investigation and class analysis.

What are the remnants of putchism and the ideology of roving rebel bands, and how can this be corrected?

The remnants of putchism and the ideology of roving rebel bands are both non-proletarian thinking that enforce a lack of discipline, laziness in political and production work, and unruly actions in the people's army.

Remnants of putschism, in particular, create adventurous and destructive actions within the people's army. These remnants are destructive in building unity within the people's army and between the people's army and the masses. They manifest through disorganized actions, a lack of discipline, burning or looting properties, and harming the masses, comrades, and prisoners.

The ideology of roving rebel bands shows through loose discipline, avoiding mass work, and seeking pleasure and recreation. For example, instead of conducting propaganda and helping with the dayto-day needs of the masses, they prefer to associate with wealthier or "fun-to-be-with" individuals to enjoy their company.

Remnants of putschism are rooted in lumpenproletarian and petit-bourgeois backgrounds. The ideology of roving rebel bands, on the other hand, is rooted in the mindset of semi-proletarians and roving lumpen-proletariats (vagabonds).

To correct these, it is important to reject their class roots. This can be accomplished through education and active ideological struggle, as well as through joining or integrating with the people's army.

j. What are the other incorrect thoughts that can be cited, according to our own experiences, and how do we combat them?

[Discuss]

Study & Proper Analysis

Revolutionary study is an important and integral part of the revolution. Comrade Mao Zedong said that "To behave like 'a blindfolded man catching sparrows,' or 'a blind man groping for fish,' to be crude and careless, to indulge in verbiage, to rest content with a smattering of knowledge—such is the extremely bad style of work that still exists among many comrades in our Party."

We need a surge in our revolutionary studies so that we can change our revolutionary movement for the better. Let us understand what revolutionary studies are and the proper way to analyze.

a. What Is Revolutionary Study?

1. Why is it important to study?

Studying is an important function, and it is the responsibility of every revolutionary to continually raise their consciousness. It is very dangerous for the masses and for the revolution to leave everything to chance. Revolutionary struggle is not an aimless struggle guided by emotions. Every action depends on concrete study of situations and the needs of the revolution. If we study situations thoroughly, we can correctly pinpoint what we need to do; we can formulate plans and determine correct methods of work in carrying them out.

Studying gives us guidance in our struggle. It doesn't just teach or show the correct road in revolutionary struggle.

It also shows us the way on how to live our everyday lives. Revolutionary studies also make us sharp in guarding against the ideas spread by the ruling class and other elements bent on seizing the revolutionary movement and leading it astray.

Revolutionary studies can be pursued by participating in collective discussions, reading revolutionary materials, ardent research, and analyzing all angles while planning and working.

Revolutionary study is a process of knowing and understanding things. It is not just the reading of theories from reading materials—like the courses and theoretical works of Marx, Lenin, Mao, and others. Proper analysis of present conditions and experiences is a very important part of revolutionary study.

The main frame of revolutionary studies is society and revolution. It involves ideas and theories that help clarify the condition of the classes and class struggle.

The reason why we study is to gather the loose ends of our struggle and change whatever it is that needs to be changed. Since we are struggling towards a free and democratic society, it is our primary concern to give importance to society and revolution. For example, we are studying the theories of classes in society and class struggle because the center, or focal point, of our struggle is understanding how to transform our society. This is the guide of how we understand the conditions of Philippine society as a whole and the continuing line of our revolutionary struggle.

Why is it important to study the People's Democratic Revolution?

We study the People's Democratic Revolution (PDR) because it shows the correct way to assess the conditions of Philippine society, the roots of the problems of the Filipino people, and the way to solve these national problems. Revolution is a science. In our fight against the reactionary enemy, we need to be sharp in studying the rules of engagement of our revolution and how the masses can fight the enemy. By studying the PDR, we can keep the zeal of our struggle both bright and fiery. We can also solidify our unity with the oppressed masses.

The basic systemic classification of the PDR can be obtained from our mass courses. Mass courses clarify for us our need to struggle. Meanwhile, in the special courses we take, we study the advancement of our mass movement—more specifically, the workers, farmers, women, and youth, as integral parts of the People's Democratic Revolution.

Revolutionaries must continuously study the PDR. While our struggle continues to intensify, our understanding of the PDR must also get sharper. The mass courses must also serve as a door to encourage us to read and study documents, journals, and books to help keep our struggle in our hearts.

The book Philippine Society and Revolution (PSR),

Struggle for National Democracy (SND), and Philippine Crisis and Revolution are the primary tools we use in studying PDR. It is where we get awareness of our questions regarding the PDR by keeping the principles of our struggle in line. This is where we get guidance in our understanding and solving the problems of our political struggle.

We read and learn Philippine history when we read the PSR. By learning the Philippine history, we also understand the advancement of Philippine society, the roots of national problems, and the revolutionary struggle for freedom and democracy. We also need to study the history, problems, and present conditions of the people of the territory in which we are currently situated.

It is very important to read Ang Bayan and other revolutionary journals to keep us abreast of the present economic and political situations and conditions of our society, its role in the revolution, and to know the struggle in other sections and territories.

What is Investigation?

Investigation is a tool to obtain proper and correct information in relation to conditions. There is Social Investigation and investigation related to work, plans, and programs.

The national social investigation is the study of classes in real life. This is a very important part of advancing our political work. In investigating the relationship of classes in the fields of economics, politics, and culture in the lives of the people, we will see a concrete picture of society, or a part of society like the community. Social investigation is important to us because it clarifies the target and ways and directions on how to arouse, organize, and mobilize the masses.

The investigation of how we conduct our work, make plans, and progress is realized by gathering data related to how we advance our work, for example, in the problems we face, the way our comrades and mass members work, and its results. Investigation is a very important part of revolutionary studies. The correct and proper information we obtain as a result of our proper investigation is important and is needed as we can formulate correct decisions, plans, and programs. Mao Zedong said, "No investigation, no right to speak." If we do not investigate, we cannot hold correct and sufficient information. As a result, whatever decision we make in taking chances will just end up frustrated.

Investigation is never-ending work. We need to make it a part of ourselves. We need to start our studies by understanding we need to have correct and enough information and data. As a result, our knowledge will always spring forth and enrich our understanding of objective conditions.

What is Analysis and Why Does It Matter?

Analysis is an important and vital part of our studies. By analyzing, we are able to determine and hit the nature and character of the things and events that we study. We are able to present its roots and are therefore able to devise ways on how to improve it.

We are able to answer the questions "Why?" "How?" and "What are its characteristics and relationships?" By following proper analysis, we are able to have a deeper understanding of facts and experiences.

Importance of Analysis in the Revolutionary Movement

Analysis is very important in the revolutionary movement. The plans and progress of the movement are based on our analysis of how to make changes to pertinent conditions and how to advance our cause. By proper analysis, we are able to clarify how to properly and effectively face and solve difficulties that arise. Through proper analysis, we are able to determine how to work more effectively and do our tasks towards victory.

The Need for Observance

We need to be observant. In whatever conditions we face, we need to be able to answer the question "What?" and most importantly "Why?" and "How?" This will help us discover the roots of the problems. We must not be subjective, imbalanced, or onesided. We must not be tricked by book covers when we analyze. We will be placed in an active position to be able to work effectively and advance our tasks.

Interconnection of Analysis and Investigation

Analysis and investigation work continuously and together. Even though they are separate activities, they are interlinked in one process. After investigating, we analyze the gathered data. We formulate conclusions and decisions that we put into practice. We again investigate how to put these into action, analyze things that we did. Based on this, we are able to formulate another conclusion and decision so we can advance even more our revolutionary tasks.

What is Assessment?

Assessment is a kind of analysis. This is an integral part of revolutionary study. There are two types of assessment that we do:

- **Assessment of Work:** Analyzing to measure where we stand or what our achievements in our plans and programs are.
- **Assessment of Conditions:** Analyzing the character of conditions and the level of class struggle in society.

An example of assessment of work is the monthly assessment that we do in preparation for reports. We list things that we've done and those things that we still need to do.

We make assessments after every mass work. We point out things that we've done from those that still need to be done; what the things that we need to complete are; the weaknesses that we need to overcome and errors that we need to rectify; and the work that we still have to do.

An example of assessment of conditions is analyzing the balance of forces—the victories of our revolutionary forces on one hand and the strength of the reactionary forces on the other. We clarify the victories of revolutionary organizing and what else we need to do to fortify and advance the revolutionary force to fight another time. We point out the strength, disposition, and movement of the enemy and how we can weaken it. By doing this, we measure our own strength in advancing the struggle and the strength of the enemy when they fight back.

Another example is how we conduct assessments on the economic conditions of farmers and farm workers in situations like after a flood, to make appropriate plans to help them in their needs.

Assessment needs to be done in a timely manner. It makes us open to the conditions and needs of the movement so that we can promptly assign tasks. Assessment gives us straight, concise, and specific tools for planning correctly and carrying out our tasks. If our constant assessment shows that conditions have changed, we need to alter our plans of action according to the changed concrete conditions.

On the other hand, assessment planning is based on the level of work we have reached. If changes and progress are pointed out during the work assessment, we change the plan and action accordingly.

What is summing up?

Summing up is analyzing both our positive and negative experiences in order to draw lessons. The conclusions we draw from our summings up are lessons that can guide us in our movement and struggle.

We learn from both positive and negative experiences. We uphold the lessons from positive experiences and consciously promote them. Meanwhile, we also learn from negative experiences but try not to repeat them again.

There are many types of summing up depending on our needs and according to the present conditions.

Situation. We mainly sum up the experiences we learn from how we mobilize the masses and lead the organization. One example is how we launch our mass campaigns. Here, we take lessons on how to correctly prepare and do mass work and conduct solid organizing in the barrios.

After gathering data and results of actions done in that particular period, we put into consideration:

a) The advance, slowing down, or reversal of the movement, then reassess the existing conditions and the lessons drawn from this.

b) The strengths, weaknesses, and mistakes in the movement, the conditions and outlook that bring these into being, and the lessons derived from it.

From this, we can learn the requirements for the optimal performance of our tasks for successful actions. The overall lesson derived from this summing up will serve as a guide for a new level of planning and action. It gives us renewed confidence to do our work and advance our struggle.

Summing up is an important part of our study. Through this, we can effectively learn from our own experiences. We can actively use these experiences, both positive and negative, to advance our knowledge and understanding of our work and responsibilities. Through summing up, we can strengthen our understanding of our revolutionary principles based on experience.

What is the complete process of analysis and revolutionary study?

Let us learn the truth from our own experiences. Mao said, "'Experiences' are all things that objectively (concretely) happen; and 'truth' is their internal cohesiveness, those laws that affect them, and 'research' is the study part."

Analyzing the condition and the struggle to change it is a continuing process. For example, we continuously research the conditions of one particular barrio or village—arouse, organize, and mobilize the masses to solve their problems. In every step and movement, we need to carefully study the conditions and the problems.

While we are still starting to penetrate one particular village, we need to study and analyze the history of the place, the nature of the terrain, what main root crop is the source of its livelihood, what the problems of the peasants are, who the local landlords and their enemy agents are, etc.

Based on the initial survey and analysis, we can make the following observations:

1. [Observation 1]
2. [Observation 2]
3. [Observation 3]

(You can fill in the specific observations or conclusions here.)

Step-by-step plans on how to arouse, organize, and mobilize the masses. We are guided by the theories of the People's Democratic Revolution, like Class Analysis.

When we act on our plans, we continue to investigate and analyze the conditions. More information is added. We are able to confirm the main conditions while we separate these from erroneous ones. We are able to analyze according to practice the results of our actions, whether these are right or wrong. We are continuously sharpening the whole condition so that we can determine and act on its changes. Based on newer, richer, and more precise ideas and conclusions, we reassess our plans and modify our actions to streamline the change we want according to the present situation. We rectify our past errors, correct false ideas and actions, and criticize wrong actions. We can also consolidate and strengthen what we concluded to be true and correct ideas and actions.

If we are able to gather enough experience, we can conclude our entire experience to be able to gather deeper lessons. These lessons will serve as guides in newer and higher stages of struggle.

An important part of this whole process is the analysis of our own strength: analysis of the whole unit in one's own struggle and condition, and the analysis of one's own struggle and each individual's work. This is where criticism and self-criticism come in.

How do we analyze things and events?

It is through analysis that we are able to deeply understand why things and events work. The conclusions that are formed by correct analysis guide us in the most important step in our study— putting it in practice. Let us therefore study how we analyze things and events.

What is the basis of correct analysis?

The correct way to analyze is based on concrete, active, true, or objective conditions and events. It means that it is not based on fantasies, dreams, rumors, superstitions, and other possibilities with no concrete basis. Concrete analysis out of concrete conditions is the only valid method to analysis.

Oftentimes, it is difficult to make the right conclusion. For example, it may be difficult to determine the true nature or cause of a problem because we are lacking concrete facts. For instance, we may be possessing incorrect or subjective data.

In this instance, there is a need to extend and deepen the investigation into the circumstances.

More often, it is hard to obtain correct conclusions even if there is enough or even more than enough data collected. In relation to this, it might also be due to the lack of applying principles learned in studies that we are not able to tie up the loose data.

It can also happen that we will generate wrong conclusions as a result of wrong analysis, even if the data is enough. By this experience, it is common that erroneous analysis is a result of wrongly processing the data.

We need to start with true, actual, and concrete data of events. Study the relationship of data, events, etc. Which is more important? Which one is not? Which one is true and which one is false? What is the chain of events?

These are the basis of true analysis.

Why do we say that all things change?

All things change. There is no way that we can say that one thing is made or complete and therefore cannot be changed. If we look at our surroundings, the environment, and society, we can see that things change, even the people. Everything has a time to be born, live, and die. There are changes that are slow and there are those that are fast. Change happens as a whole, continual process from its birth to its death.

Many people believe that a lot of things cannot change or are impossible to be changed. One reason is that all change is not easy to see; it takes a long process to see the expected change. This idea is usually spread by the ruling class. For example, they say that it is impossible to change the condition between the rich and the poor in society.

We know that this is not true and that this idea is spread by the ruling and oppressive class so that they can keep the masses from waging revolution.

Many also believe that if things change, it is simply a transfer of position, an increase in numbers, or a repetition. For example, the only things seen in the history or development of society are the migration of people, population increase, the change of a new generation, or the actions of

"Great leaders." Such a view denies the underlying or revolutionary changes taking place in history, such as changes in the economic, political, and cultural systems of society.

A person's knowledge is a byproduct of their constant study of change and movement. A person's progress is their knowledge proportionate to the progress in society. There is an advancement in one's knowledge in analysis, coexistent with one's understanding of the reason for change. It is only through one's progress in one's knowledge that one can actively and effectively do things to advance one's revolutionary work.

This also helps a person find a way out of difficult situations by having an iron will to press on in the face of problems and difficult situations. This teaches us that if we correctly assess our conditions, we will be able to understand how we will solve each problem and difficult situation that will come our way.

What are the reasons why things change?

Everything has two opposing forces that continue to fight. This is called contradiction. The character of things is dictated by contradictions, and the progression and change in things are also dictated by the constant struggle of power within the given contradiction. Therefore, change in things is internal and not external.

For example, why does Philippine society advance and change? Is it fate that dictates it? The climate of the land? Is it help from other territories? No. Change in society is a result of its internal contradictions: the struggle of its classes. On one side is the ruling and oppressive class that prevents the advancement of the country, and on the other side is the oppressed class that demands progress, freedom, and democracy.

External conditions influence change. Nothing exists that is separate from its surroundings. Its movement is relative to other things that exist that can either hasten or slow its progress.

For example, our comrade's progress is a result of the continuing internal struggle between correct and wrong ideas. In the fight for the national and democratic aspirations of the people versus anything that wants to oppose it, it is up to each comrade to press on with the revolutionary struggle or just be passive and do nothing. However, there are other important external influences that may affect the given comrade: his collective, family and loved ones, the masses he meets in his area, etc.

In the first example, the progress of Philippine society rests primarily on the struggle of the people against US imperialism, feudalism, and bureaucrat capitalism that is sharply mirrored by the revolution. The advance and victory of the revolution cannot be based on external forces like the victory of the struggle in other countries or the help of other comrades. Though the conducive external conditions and the help of other comrades to the Philippine revolution are important and can definitely help us attain our goals of revolutionary victory.

This understanding teaches us to be wary or not to be skin-deep in our analysis. To be able to understand one thing, we must be able to study its internal character and its relationship to other things. We must be able to study the data we collected and separate what is right from what is wrong. We must be able to study the internal contradictions and how they are influenced by the external contradictions.

Why do we say "divide one into two" is the correct way to analyze?

The correct method of analysis? "Dividing one into two" simply means studying the contradictions in things. This is going to the core of things, to study its character and opposition between aspects of contradictions. We study its movement and progress, its forms, and the ways by which contradictions struggle, bits rise and fall, action and counter-action, etc. This is the proper way to study.

This reminds us not to be one-sided in our analysis. Being one-sided means only looking at one aspect of a thing or contradiction. This also means favoring one aspect of the contradiction. This may also mean laziness in studying the two aspects of contradiction and how the two oppose each other.

For example, when we criticize a comrade, we look at her or his positive and negative characteristics. In our investigation of one barrio, we study the peasants and farm workers on the one hand and the landlord on the other hand. In our analysis of society, we both look at the exploited and oppressed classes and the exploiting and oppressing classes.

To know the essence or nature of one thing, we must know which among its two aspects acts as its principal. This is important because the principal aspect is the one that dictates the nature of things.

Whatever we analyze, we must immediately center on its very nature: studying the contradictions, studying its opposing force and character that dictates its movement, and determining which aspect acts as the principal one.

With our comrades, for example, we analyze the contradictions of their way of thinking, both positive and negative, the revolutionary from the non-revolutionary. We can therefore clearly define the principal character—the positive, correct, and revolutionary.

When we analyze our movement, we also analyze:

- What we've so far accomplished
- Things we still have to do
- At what level we have met our goal
- Our strengths and weaknesses

We also need to point out which one stands out.

In analyzing the contradictions, we use the help of comparison and differentiating it from other contradictions. The contradictions in one barrio, for example, can be compared and differentiated with the contradictions of other barrios. By comparing, we are able to analyze the common character that is present in the contradiction we are studying and in those other contradictions. This will help us to immediately focus on analyzing the essence of things, which helps us understand further the similarities and differences in contradictions and things.

In differentiating, we are able to study different characteristics present in other contradictions. In differentiating, we are able to form and beef up our understanding of the things we analyze. This is important to enable us to generate accurate and appropriate solutions for how we should act.

For example, when we analyze an agricultural community, we know that its contradictions are the same as those of the rest of the agricultural communities in the Philippines. That is why it is very important to wage the agrarian revolution in the barrio, and studying the experience of other places that we read in Ang Bayan can help us fulfill that goal.

On the other hand, there are different forms and ways of land rent and usury, the power of influence of the landlords, and of the overseer. The military force varies, and the size and strength of the mass movement in the barrio and the readiness of the masses vary too. That is why it is not good to copy all the steps employed by other territories in lowering the land rent.

It is important to know our history.

Investigate our comrade; we investigate their class background, their family, how they got involved, and the history of their struggle. When we analyze Philippine society, it is very important to know its history, to know the historical root of its current condition, to enable us to understand its basic character.

"Dividing one into two" is the proper way to conduct an analysis. We first try to study and learn the two aspects that form the contradiction, and then we try to determine which one is the dominant or principal one. We compare things from one to

the other to know the essence that is common to both of them. We also need to study how the contradictions thrive in them.

What is the main force that affects change on an object?

The effect or process that we study is complicated. It means that it has different contradictions. We need to study its different contradictions—the two aspects of contradictions and the relationship of these contradictions with one another—to prevent us from becoming one-sided.

Among its many contradictions, there is one that is decisive to the object and process. The contradiction is the common denominator that strings, connects, and affects the progress of other contradictions. It is therefore the key to understand the character of one particular complicated thing or process and how it exists and flourishes.

We first need to study different contradictions before we know the principal contradiction. It is one-sided and subjective to study only one contradiction even though this is the principal or decisive contradiction. It is not clear if it can indeed be the principal contradiction if we cannot see how it is related to the other existing contradictions.

For example, there will be many contradictions when we investigate one particular barrio. There will be the contradiction between rich peasants, poor peasants, and farm workers. There will be the contradiction between the landlords and rich peasants. There will be the contradiction between the peasants and businessmen. There will be contradictions between peasants themselves.

In this barrio, the principal contradiction is between the landlord on the one hand and the tenants and farm workers on the other hand. This is the main force that influences the other contradictions in the barrio. It is also important to study other contradictions to enable us to see the whole picture and how these contradictions relate to one another.

In simple things and processes, the principal or dominant aspect of a contradiction determines the nature of a thing. In complex things or processes, understanding the interplay of various contradictions is crucial.

In complex processes, the principal aspect of the principal contradiction is the main determining factor of the nature of a thing, of its essence.

In the given example, the landlord has an upper hand over the tenants and farm workers. He can conduct usury and dictate the rent for the land and the salary he wants to give to the tenants and farm workers. This can influence the other contradictions. This condition can be the basis for the abuse and oppression between the businessperson or usurer and the poor farmers and farm workers. The influence of the big landlord can define the character and condition of the barrio we are investigating.

By knowing the principal contradiction, we clear the way for us to solve other lesser contradictions. In the example mentioned, we face the struggle between the rich peasants, on the one hand, and the poor peasants and the farm workers, on the other, in relation to the destruction of the big landlord. Meaning, we are able to neutralize them and not overly hurt their interests so that they are not going to side with the landlord and instead support the struggle of the poor farmers and farm workers.

We learn from this that in complex things and processes that have a lot of contradictions, the principal contradiction is the decisive factor in the way things work, and the principal aspect of the principal contradiction is the primary factor in the nature of a thing. This teaches us that in analysis, we study the contradictions that comprise the object; analyze contradictions as to which is the primary one and how it strongly influences other contradictions; and study the aspects and define which among the two aspects is the principal. We also need to study secondary contradictions and their aspects.

Why is it necessary to consider the relationship of the whole and its parts?

When we analyze something, we need to relate it to the whole so that we won't become one-sided and be biased in the decisions that we draw. On the other hand, we must be able to form and place everything in a much deeper context if we are to critically analyze its parts.

Everything that we analyze is part of a greater whole. We need to relate the relationship of things we study in its "wholeness." We need to point out how it influences the progress of the whole.

Doing this, we will be able to better understand how things evolve.

For example, one barrio that we control is part of the municipality and province. If there is a province-wide increase in military presence, it is also reflected or felt in the barrio that we control in the presence of CAFGUs and an increase in military operations.

Another example is the movement of our group and the organizing committee in the barrio. The plans that we make depend on the plans of the section and district. In our assessment, we take notice of the effect and influence of our guides as we move along with other works in the given municipality and section.

Our analysis must also give importance to the study of its parts. We need to be more conclusive and deep in our understanding and evade shallow analysis.

When we analyze, it is not enough to say that we are good in the overall movement of our work. We need to deeply assess the flow of different groups and the way we do our tasks in educating, organizing, and mobilizing the masses. By doing this, our analysis will be clearer and more realistic according to our plans and programs.

Another example is our way of assessing the mass work of a particular organizing group in a particular barrio. This kind of analysis will give us a better picture of the whole by clearly understanding its parts.

How do things change?

There is contradiction from the beginning to the end of everything. It is important to study the progress of contradictions in the whole process to be able to understand and point to the character of things and how it proceeds. Progress advances quantitatively and qualitatively.

At first, one aspect of the contradiction weighs more than the other corresponding aspect. This dominant aspect is the one that gives character to the thing. The Philippines, for example, is semifeudal and semi-colonial because it is being governed by US imperialism, feudalism, and bureaucrat capitalism.

But this is not eternal. Contradictions exist.

Change and strength continue to exist and influence the two contradictory forces, can sometimes be seen, and at times are hidden. This is quantitative change. We seem not to see the change but often only see simple changes in the form or the outward conditions of things. There may also be no change in the position.

For example, in the Philippines, the class struggle can be seen in changes such as the increase in unemployment, the escalation in the number of strikes and other forms of actions, and an increase in the strength of the people's army and so on. The people continue to fight the exploitation and oppression that is being forced upon them by the State. Meanwhile, the ruling class continues to intensify their exploitation and oppression and its abuse and deception towards the marginalized sector and the people. The intensity of the struggle and the balance of forces continue to change, but not the condition of society. No changes occur in the basic relationship in the classes of society. That's one reason why Philippine society will remain semi-feudal and semi-colonial.

There will be a qualitative change if there's a change in position between two aspects. If the secondary aspect continues to surge forward, there will come a time that the primary aspect will become weaker and will be overrun by the secondary historically weak aspect. This change can be sudden and drastic. This is called a degree of qualitative change. The exchange of position of dominance in the conflicting aspects will usher in a leap that changes the nature of things. Now there is a new dominant aspect in the nature of things.

As a result of the change in the balance of forces, qualitative change in the current Filipino society will come after the victory of the national democratic revolution. The classes that used to rule, oppress, and exploit will now be ruled, and the classes that once were ruled, oppressed, and exploited will now rule. There will be a revolutionary change in Philippine society, fundamental changes in the politics, economy, and culture of the people.

We need to analyze what the quantitative change serves. The quantitative change that serves the principal aspect will not lead to qualitative change. At the same time, the quantitative changes that serve the secondary aspect will lead to qualitative changes.

Let us look at reforms, for example. Reformism is different from revolutionary struggle.

Reforms only bring surface-level changes and do not contribute to bringing changes in the basic structure of society. At times, it can even bring delay. Meanwhile, the revolutionary struggle for reforms, while working for change, makes the revolution stronger and serves the revolutionary change. The difference can even be seen in the goals and means of bringing in the type of issues and struggles. For example—an increase in the price of farm products and the fight against the increase in oil prices; reformism does not go to the root of the problem of why this is happening and the relationship of the State to these problems.

In addition, we are able to classify the quantitative and qualitative changes to advance qualitative changes in things and events.

For example, in organizing a union in a factory, we need to estimate if our organizing level is enough or not so that we can decide if we can openly fight and forward the struggle to project our union. At the same time, we also need to estimate if farmer groups have enough strength to face oppressive companies to lessen rent on the land. If the analysis is poorly done, we might get into a struggle that we are not capable of winning, or we will waver in our decision to enter a struggle that is actually within our reach.

Another example. In the process of advancing the People's Democratic Revolution, the revolutionary forces should, step-by-step, gather strength while we weaken the reactionary enemy at the same time. It needs to attain the level of political and military strength that the balance will turn to the level where we are ready to grab political power. To dream of premature military victory without first readying the political maturity will surely give us failure.

Proper understanding teaches us how things change, their progress towards quantitative and qualitative changes, the proper analysis of the form and strength of the opposing forces, the intensity of contradiction, recognizing how quantitative leads to qualitative changes, and the understanding of how conditions can be used to attain qualitative changes.

How do we solve contradictions?

The character of one thing changes as there's a qualitative change that occurs between the principal and secondary aspects of the contradiction. Conflicting conditions inside the contradictions end. This gives way to new contradictions and new things with new conditions. As new aspects form out of the old ones, quality changes and becomes something new.

For example, the semi-feudal and semi-colonial character of Philippine society will change in the victory of the People's Democratic Revolution and in the defeat of the armed power of US imperialism, comprador bourgeoisie, and big landlords. The aforementioned rotten and reactionary aspects previously dominant throughout Philippine society will become secondary, and the Filipino people and the revolutionary leadership of the working class and its Party will be in control.

The result will be the dismantling of the semi feudal and semi-colonial state of the Philippines and the ushering in of a socialist society.

Another example: we promote the Agrarian Revolution in solving the contradictions between the rich landlords and the farm workers. If we are able to maximize enforcing the agrarian reform program, we are able to solve the contradictions, dismantle the landlord form of power, and will be able to erase feudalism. At the same time, new problems will sprout up in relation to agricultural cooperation and collectivization.

It is a vital part of our studies to understand how to solve these contradictions. The contradictions that differ in quality can be solved using different qualitative ways. For example, the contradictions between the rich landlords and farm workers can only be solved by the agrarian revolt; the contradiction between the imperialists and landlords versus the toiling Filipino people can only be solved by employing the People's Democratic Revolution. The struggle between the farmers and farm workers can be solved by increasing the salary according to the level of struggle against feudalism; and the contradiction between the people can be solved by clarifying what is right from what is wrong.

The things we assess are those that continue to move, progress, and change. Our understanding of how things change is very important to be able to make a proper analysis. Let us retrace a little bit. All things change, and the reason why it changes is inside of it, in its contradictions and the internal struggle of the opposing aspects that exist throughout the process from its beginning to its end. External forces can influence it and stand in the way of change. The principal aspect of the

Contradiction determines the nature of the thing.

A simple object can be complicated and can be made up of different contradictions, and the principal contradiction determines the primary character of the object. The contradiction never stops and goes through a gradual period and qualitative change. The secondary aspect gets stronger and the primary aspect gets weaker over time until it reaches the point where there is a complete change in position. This is the qualitative change, the change in the nature of things. The old contradiction gets solved. A new one emerges.

This teaches us the proper way to analyze—going back to a concrete basis, "dividing one into two parts"; classifying the internal and external parts; the necessity of studying all contradictions that compose one complicated matter; pointing out the principal contradiction and its principal aspect to know the character of things; the relationship between the primary and secondary contradictions; pointing at the principal and secondary aspects of every contradiction and how they struggle; how quantitative change occurs; how the whole represents the parts; and how the contradictions get solved, giving way to newer contradictions. To this effect, we will be able to understand not just the character and nature of things, but also how we can change it. In short, this teaches us the importance of concrete analysis in concrete conditions.

Why is it that "the masses, and the masses only, are the makers of history" is the guiding principle of the mass line?

The principle "The masses, and the masses only, are the makers of history" is a principle born out of scientific means using deep analysis of human history. Comrade Mao said, "The masses, and the masses alone, are the motive force of world history." Many centuries of human history time and again have shown that it is the masses that create change in society.

- It is through their work in production that feeds society.
- It is through their brains and brawn that bring progress to society in general.
- It is through their collective strength that prevents any force that wants to undermine the progress of society.

These problems in society can be manifested in forms of economic crisis whose brunt is mostly borne by the toiling masses. If you cannot move the masses, there will be no underlying change in society. This is what is meant when we say the masses are the real heroes.

The principle "the masses, and the masses only, are the makers of history" is the basic principle of the mass line because it explains in a scientific manner why we need to fully trust the masses and why we have to arouse, organize, and mobilize the masses for revolutionary struggle and in advancing our revolutionary tasks.

What does it mean that we need to trust and rely on the masses?

We must firmly grasp within ourselves that the Revolution is one endeavor shared by the wide mass of people. If the masses do not actively participate, the victory of the revolution can never be achieved. We need to trust the masses, especially the farmers and workers, to win the People's Democratic Revolution.

It is through the active participation and action of the masses that we can achieve our revolutionary aims and solve the problems that will come.

Along the way, there is therefore a need to go to the masses, unite with them, and effectively lead them. It is through persistent and continuous arousing, organizing, and mobilizing of the masses that we can concretize to them the strength of our revolutionary ideas that will become a powerful material that will push the movement of society for the better.

Lesson III - The Mass Line

Comrade Mao said, we need "to be good at translating the Party's policy into action of the masses, to be good at getting not only the leading cadres but also the broad masses to understand and master every movement and every struggle we launch."

What do close and warm relationships with the masses mean?

The mass line means that we should maintain a close relationship with the masses. First, we need to integrate in our hearts the interests of the masses.

We need to make sure that all comrades are tightly connected to the masses and place their interests above all things. The mass line teaches us that we must love the masses at all times. We must always listen to them and integrate with them instead of putting ourselves above them.

In integrating with the masses, we are able to arouse them and elevate their level of understanding, help them learn how to organize themselves, and collate all essentials in their present condition and struggle. We need to give notice to the interests of the masses; their basic problems like landlessness, high rents, low wages, etc.—all these, and even their particular problems like lack of rice to eat, salt to give flavor to their food, etc. We need to assess these problems and make proper decisions related to these problems.

By doing this, we can show the masses that we embody their interests and our lives are connected to theirs. It is through this understanding that we can help them understand bigger tasks related to the advancement of the revolutionary struggle towards victory.

Nothing will happen to the struggles of one leading group if it is not closely related and combined in the action of the masses that can only be realized through a close relationship with them. On the other hand, if only the masses move without the strong leadership of the Party, they cannot sustain that struggle nor steer it in the proper direction or raise it to a higher level of revolutionary struggle.

What does "from the masses to the masses" mean?

The proper way to lead the masses is **"from the masses, to the masses."** This means that we need to collate the fragmented ideas and thoughts of the masses and mold them properly. We need to return and explain to the masses the formed idea until they understand and accept it.

The mass line agrees with the "from the masses, to the masses" leadership. We depend on the intellect and knowledge of the masses to understand their conditions and problems so that we can generate ideas on how to solve them. Correct planning and decisions can be made if they are part of the experience of the masses. It is therefore our role to go to the masses and immerse ourselves in their midst to gather the different lines of thinking of the masses we want to serve. In analyzing and summing up these ideas, we can concentrate them into one systematic whole that mirrors an objective condition and intellect of the masses.

We need to rely on the capability and strength of the masses if we want to help them solve their basic problems. We trust that however big the problem is, we can solve it as long as the masses have unity and collective decisions. It is then our responsibility to let the masses understand that the ideas that are formed are the results of their very own ideas, and they need to embrace them as their own and realize them through collective action.

What does it mean that we need to act and move according to the interest and readiness of the masses?

The mass line teaches us that we need to struggle according to the objective interest of the masses. This means that we need to move according to their concrete conditions and needs, not according to what we think. We will get separated from the masses even if our intentions are good if we deviate from their objective interests. In general, the tasks and protocols we establish are correct if they align with what the masses want according to the present time and space.

At first, the masses may not be aware of their objective needs and do not realize the need for change or are not yet ready to take a step for that change. If we do not present our ideas in a timely manner, however correct they may be, we will separate ourselves from them. We need to be patient and persistent in the way we explain things to the masses until they are ready to accept these ideas based on concrete conditions and the masses themselves are ready to act.

Work for the change that they want.

We need to be guarded against **commandism**—this means overestimating the actual political awareness of the masses and violating the voluntary movement of the masses. Comrades will only discover the level of preparedness of the masses if they go to the ranks of the masses and conduct an investigation.

On the other hand, we also need to be wary of **tailism** of the masses. This means slow progression of their level of political consciousness and the backwardness of their level of struggle for revolutionary change. Some comrades may be following some slow elements; it is wrong to think that their views are the views of the whole broad masses.

To be able to destroy commandism and tailism, we need to bring ourselves closer to the basic masses and conduct proper investigation and analysis. How do we do this?

We can divide the masses into three parts:

1. **The Advanced**: These ranks of the masses have a clear understanding of their basic conditions and are ready to struggle to change it.

2. **The Middle**: This part may understand the need for change but are reluctant and hesitant to move for action.
3. **The Backward**: These can be easily influenced by backward ways of thinking and may be resistant to struggle for change.

We trust the advanced elements of the mass movement. It is through them that we are able to make the middle force move and can even coax some of the backward forces. This way, we are able to lead the masses according to their objective interest, depending on their readiness to struggle for change.

If we do not depend on the readiness of the masses, we might surpass their basic political consciousness and awareness. We might make them move by ordering them around, and not by their free will according to their understanding. At the same time, if we tie ourselves to the greater numbers but backward masses, we will be tailing instead of leading them. It might happen that the advanced and middle masses are ready and are calling to struggle for change, and it ends up that the Party is the one that needs convincing.

We need to be consistent in elevating the revolutionary consciousness of the masses. This means that we need to be at the forefront in giving revolutionary education so that the masses will continue to advance.

Continue to elevate their level of readiness to struggle and fight. In relation to this, we are also able to strengthen, solidify, and broaden the organized strength of the masses so that there will be an elevated level of their struggle towards victory.

Why is the propagation of the line of the People's Democratic Revolution the key in giving life to the mass line in the current period of the Philippine revolution?

The line of the People's Democratic Revolution (PDR) was formed from studying the history and conditions of Philippine society. This answers the interest of the nation for freedom and democracy. The PDR springs from the objective conditions and needs of the masses and points towards the path of revolutionary change. Because it follows the objective interest of the masses, the line of the PDR is easily understood by the masses and is easily embraced as their own.

The line of the PDR is the key to effectively arouse, organize, and mobilize the millions of exploited masses. In studying the particular conditions, problems, and outlooks of the masses in the area of discipline, we need to guide it according to the line of the PDR.

Why is the democratic style of work important in living the mass line?

Aside from the correct line of the PDR that we employ in our everyday practice, the democratic style of work is important in living the mass line. Experience clearly shows us that the correct style of work strengthens our connection to the masses, while the wrong style of work runs opposite to the wishes and needs of the masses in an established time, which may be a reason for our detachment from the masses.

We need to make decisions after we do proper investigation and consultation with other comrades and masses and after proper collective discussions. It is not enough that only the leadership understands the decision that was made. We need to convey it to the masses and make them understand so that they can be active participants in following these decisions.

We need to effectively unite as one majority with the comrades and the masses. We need to listen to the masses and accept the correct observations and criticize what is erroneous. We need to avoid working in small groups. We need to cultivate the democratic style of work at all times.

Why does the mass line correspond to the revolutionary class line?

Who composes the Filipino masses? Who are the masses that need to be aroused, organized, and mobilized? These questions can be answered only if we analyze the classes and understand the revolutionary class line.

The revolutionary class line is the principle that teaches us to know the dynamics and relationship of classes in Philippine society. It teaches us who are the friends from the enemies of the revolution and who are the exploited and oppressed classes. It also clarifies the correct class analysis of how we can lead the masses:

trusting the advanced ranks of the masses, encouraging the middle forces, and separating and fighting the enemies. We also take advantage of the strife among the enemy so that we can further weaken the ruling class and strengthen our own revolutionary forces.

Overall, the revolutionary class line teaches us to give importance to the strength of the working class, the peasants, and the semi-proletariat. In the countryside, we give importance to the advanced ranks of farm workers and the poor and lowermiddle peasants. We also bring into the fold the middle and upper-middle peasants and neutralize the rich peasants. We also take advantage of the strife occurring among the enlightened and despotic landlords. Through this, we can effectively separate and weaken the landlord class. It is through the revolutionary class line that there can be a scientific way of recognizing who composes the masses in one particular place.

Lesson IV

Democratic Centralism & the Committee System

Democratic Centralism

What is an organization and why is it important?

An organization is a system that groups together people to stand and act as one effective force. It binds members and parts to move as one in advancing one unified goal. It is through an organization and organized action that unity based in one spirit and zeal can have a concrete form of expression.

As a system, an organization has strong principles that guide its members on how to think and act. It has its own set of rules and objectives that are mirrored by its system of leadership with different levels of responsibility. These are necessary elements that make it certain the organization marches to one drumbeat and cadence in achieving its goal.

We can compare the organization to a broom that gets its strength when we tie its fronds together. If the fronds are separate, it is weak and can easily be broken. But if tied together, it becomes an effective tool to clean dirt.

What is a revolutionary organization? Why is it important?

An organization is classified as revolutionary if it promotes the interest of the broad masses. It is intent on struggling to free the people from exploitation towards genuine change in society. The history of Philippine society is full of experiences of Filipinos forming different organizations to forward their revolutionary struggle. For example, the Katipunan was formed in 1896 as an armed force or army of the people in their fight against Spanish colonial rule. At present, there are the Communist Party of the Philippines, the New People's Army, and various mass organizations in different corners of the country that are struggling to achieve national freedom and genuine democracy.

In contrast, there are different organizations built by the enemy. These reactionary organizations are bent on cuddling and catering to the interests of the exploitative and oppressive classes. The enemy wants to maintain the present status of society where only a few get the benefits of the land. Direct and indirect methods are used to deceive and oppress the people. There are the AFP, the Barrio Councils, and bogus cooperatives.

Not only do these favor the enemy, but they also make sure that the toiling masses are fragmented. The enemy utilizes the "divide and conquer" tactic to dismantle the formation of our unity. This is the reason why the ruling class, who are few in number, can control the majority of the Filipino people. As long as we are fragmented, we are not going to be effective in fighting the exploitation, oppression, and domination of the ruling class. But if we are organized and have strong unity, like a broom, we can remove the dirt and problems of our society. The strength of our unity is the only force that the majority of the oppressed Filipino people use in its fight against the powerful enemy.

This is the reason why it is our responsibility to form revolutionary organizations so that our unity and struggle can continuously flow. We must always make sure that we augment and strengthen our roles and excel in binding and mobilizing our forces. It is only through this that we can concretize the majority of the strength and power of the exploited and oppressed classes to overthrow their class enemies and build a democratic and free Philippines.

Being a member of a revolutionary mass organization is voluntary. Membership means being determined and committed to the cause of the organization and consciously embracing the principles, policies, and decisions of the organization.

What is democratic centralism?

Democratic centralism is the principle that guides us in forming and making our organization work. This ensures that we will act as one unified organization.

Democratic centralism means that centralism is based on democracy and democracy guided by centralized leadership.

- **Centralism based on democracy**: All must emphasize the general interest of the organization. An effective organization draws its strength from the active participation of all its members and parts. Decisions are collectively discussed based on the overall interest of the group.

- **Democracy guided by centralized leadership**: The individual interest and action are subordinate to, and agree with, the overall interests and goals of the organization. The decision of the organization is tightly followed, and everyone is free to work towards the organization's interests and goals.

The overall essence of centralism depends on the strong commitment of each member to the principles and objectives of the organization that unify the whole membership. Member discipline stems from this commitment, which is essential to the organization's success.

On the other hand, democracy means the involvement of members in forming, upholding, and working on the decisions, and the conscious effort of each member in fulfilling their roles and rights as members of the organization.

The principle of democratic centralism makes it clear how we can have a vibrant and efficient way to struggle. As a result, we can make the right decisions, plans, and programs and know how to make them work. Following democratic centralism assures us that our organization will remain strong despite all efforts of the enemy to destroy it. Living and embodying the principles of democratic centralism is important to ensure an organized way of carrying our revolution towards victory.

At its core, democratic centralism involves strictly upholding the basic principles and implementing the policies and decisions of the organization. This is the primary way to ensure unity in thought and action of all members.

What are the basic conditions for establishing democratic centralism?

We need the following conditions to give life to democratic centralism:

a) The leading units and groups at all levels of the organization are chosen democratically. They are responsible to the group that chose them for the positions.

b) After a free and thorough discussion, all decisions of the group are enforced and expected to be followed without hesitation according to the four principles of discipline.

c) The leading unit or group must thoroughly read reports and inputs from the group and masses they lead. They must always study the concrete experiences of the conditions and be immediate in giving guidance to solving problems that may arise.

d) The lower units must give regular and special reports about their work to the higher organs, and they must proactively ask for instructions on problems that may arise and require decisions from the higher organs.

e) All units follow the principles of collective leadership, and all important discussions are collectively decided.

What are the four principles of discipline?

The four principles of discipline are important to assure the unity of our organization. These are based on the principle of democratic centralism. These are:

1. **The individual is subject to the organization.** This means that every individual member's interest must be subordinate to the interest of the organization. She or he needs to follow the Constitution of the organization and its decisions without protest.
2. **The minority is subordinated to the majority.** This means that all organizational decisions are based on the agreement made by the majority. Even if there is a small group that poses a different opinion after the organization has already handed down its decision, this minority must follow and adhere to the collective decision.
3. **The lower level is subject to the higher level.** This means that the lower unit or group must follow the decisions and functions of the higher organ, which represents a wider field of the organization.

4. **The entire membership is under the highest level of leadership or congress.** This means that all decisions and policies formed by the top leadership and the congress must be observed by all members and parts of the organization.

What are the responsibilities of leadership at the higher levels of the organization?

The revolutionary organization has a different type of leadership compared to the bourgeois or feudal type of organization in the current corrupt society. They are not like kings that just order around their territory. The leadership is composed and moves according to the principles of democratic centralism. It moves according to the interest of the whole organization and not just for the interest of an individual or a smaller group or unit.

The leadership is democratically selected. It may be done via a simple consensus of members towards the elected leadership or, if the organization is ready enough due to rich experience, through an electoral process.

The leadership's primary role is to lead the organization. It watches the overall function of the whole organization to ensure it is working on advancing the goals of the organization. It directly leads in working on important tasks to make sure it advances the decisions, plans, and programs of action.

Functions of Leadership

One important function of leadership is to draft the plans and programs of action of the organization. The particular goals of one given period and the list of tasks that need to be done are normally written in the program. The leadership must also establish rules and regulations on how to successfully work on these plans.

It is through progress and plans of action that we are able to systematize and unify the progress of our organization. It is then necessary that our progress and actions are related to the objective interest of the masses. The plans and programs that were drafted must be immediately presented and explained to all members.

It is important that the leadership can control the movement of the whole organization and even its parts. The leadership receives reports from the lower organs of the organization and studies these reports. The leadership also goes directly to the ranks of members and the masses and directly gathers necessary information to know the concrete conditions. Through this, the leadership can immediately act on any change in the conditions.

The organization is prompt in guiding, deciding, and solving any problem that will exist. As a result, it can ensure that the tasks can always advance.

General Assembly

The leadership calls and conducts the general assembly of the organization. This is where important points involving the vital interests and actions of the organization are discussed and decided. This is also where the leadership reports to the assembly the conditions and order of action of the whole organization so that proper decisions can be made if necessary. It is the leadership's responsibility to ensure that unity is successfully met inside these meetings.

Responsibilities of Members and Lower Organs

The membership of a revolutionary organization is composed of active and responsible individuals who work to advance the goals of the organization. This is different from the members of any bourgeois or feudal organizations with loose unity that only follow the dictates of their leaders or who hope to use leverage to be offered.

Leadership roles in a revolutionary organization do not operate according to self-interest or that of a small group but for the organization as a whole. Each individual member works to solidify and form an organization that will fight the ruling class.

Every individual member has the responsibility to:

- Follow all decisions

- Uphold all tasks and plans
- Advance to the best of their ability
- Ensure the security of the group
- Move according to the overall interest of the organization

It is necessary for all members to study the decisions, plans, and programs to fully understand them and determine how to act properly and direct ways on how to work. The leadership must immediately address any questions and problems as a result of the work.

All members and lower units of the organization have the responsibility to regularly send their reports along with their suggestions, observations, and criticisms on important issues affecting the organization. It is every member's responsibility to study their condition intently and honestly provide correct information. This is crucial for devising proper plans and decisions.

It is also the individual member's responsibility to attend meetings, help ensure unity, and assist in making decisions. Members share their experiences and knowledge in meetings and actively voice their opinions, observations, suggestions, and feedback.

B. The Committee System

What is collective leadership?

Collective leadership involves practicing the principles of democratic centralism in leading a revolutionary organization. It teaches how the leading committee can guide the collective. All important points are collectively decided and implemented.

Through collective leadership, membership can be democratically represented in the leadership with broad-based democratic participation. The leadership can more effectively identify the difficulties the organization faces, strengthening and unifying the leadership committee in guiding the revolutionary organization.

It is also through collective leadership that other representatives and the excellent actions of members can combine their responsibilities in leading the organization. This strengthens the initiative of every member to participate in making and enacting the decisions of the collective. This can prevent the monopoly of one or more sections in the general decision-making and route of action of the organization.

What is the committee system?

The committee system is a system or way of collective action of the leading group or committee. We can see in the committee system the sharing of work, the relationship between the secretary and the members, how to conduct a meeting, etc. It aims to strengthen the leadership of the organization so that it can effectively act on its leadership responsibilities.

The committee system is important and needs to be studied and effectively put into practice. This is a way to effectively put into action the principles of collective leadership. Especially in the growth and development of the tasks of the leadership of the growing organization, you need to take into consideration the organized and systematic way of how the entire organization works.

The committee system effectively combines collective leadership and individual responsibility. The effective action of every member in the committee in their particular duties helps strengthen the collective leadership.

The committee system also helps prevent problems that can slow or even stop the movement of the whole committee. If there's a systematized way in dividing tasks, we can prevent the dumping of work onto the secretariat while the rest of the membership does nothing. If there is a systematic way to conduct a meeting, we can prevent frequent and long, arduous meetings and can even prepare for each and every meeting. We can prevent neglecting other important tasks. We can also effectively solve problems in a timely manner. The committee system is important so that the committee can effectively face important tasks and problems of leadership.

3. What is the responsibility of the secretary?

The secretary heads the committee. In other words, he or she is the leader of the committee's collective action.

The secretary is the main person who follows the committee's action. The secretary always makes sure that the committee effectively works on all its tasks. They make sure that the committee does not just monitor but elevates its collective action to a higher level. They guide the work of every member in putting into practice the collective decision. She or he immediately investigates and consults with the members on any problem or change in conditions that needs to be acted upon.

The secretary leads the committee in following decisions and solving problems that may arise. They are placed in a vital position to center on and bind the collective action of the committee, continually unifying the membership. Through this, they can ensure the unified march of the members to effectively lead the organization's actions.

Proper Relationship Between the Secretary and the Members of the Committee

Tight unity must exist between the secretary and the members of the committee: the unity to follow their leadership responsibilities given to them by the organization. This unity is important for effective leadership. An important element is the trust between the members to maintain the unity of the whole committee.

As a leader of the committee, the secretary follows the action of the members, ensuring they efficiently implement the committee's decisions. They guide and help each member in their work. By leading by example, they demonstrate the proper way to work. However, they are not above or unique from the committee and its members. The secretary's voice and rights are the same as the members, with no special privileges, and it is their responsibility to follow collective decisions.

It is the members' task and responsibility to support and help the secretary. This is done with respect to the leadership of the secretary. Such support and respect are effective conditions in helping the secretary do their work, especially if there are problems and changes in conditions that need action. Each member contributes to monitoring any trends and actions of the organization and the committee. They help in preparing and announcing meetings. Inside the meetings, members help ensure they run smoothly and assist in solving misunderstandings or disputes. They also take the initiative in any work and do not just wait for the secretary.

Responsibilities of the Deputy-Secretary

The position of the deputy-secretary is a way of showing joint effort and sharing of work inside the committee. It supports the secretary so that the latter can address more important problems and responsibilities.

The deputy-secretary will perform the duties of the secretary if the latter cannot fulfill their role for any reason. This ensures that the committee will not stagnate if the secretary cannot effectively lead.

It is fine to have one deputy-secretary if the organization is new or small. As the organization grows, so do its committees and work. It is then proper to place deputy-secretaries in different divisions of work. We can assign deputy-secretaries to areas such as organization, education, finance, etc., depending on the needs of the organization.

The secretary and the deputy-secretary compose the secretariat. The secretariat effectively leads the everyday actions of the committees. The secretariat does not differ from the leadership, nor is it above a committee.

What needs to be considered to make sure that meetings run smoothly?

Meetings are an important part of committee action. This is where decisions are made on advancing the goals of the organization. In meetings, the committee collectively discusses making decisions, plans, and programs of action. Meetings give life to the collective leadership and the unity of the committee. It is the committee's task to set up and follow a system of meetings.

- **Scheduling:** Meetings ought to be scheduled regularly by the committee. Avoid conducting meetings too often. The higher organ tasks and the committee can estimate how often the organization will assess work, prepare reports, program, and plan, among other things.

- **Duration:** We must avoid long meetings. This can happen if our organization seldom meets, or if meetings are not adequately prepared and/or effectively led. If needed, conduct special meetings to decide on issues that arise and need immediate resolution.
- **Preparation:** Make sure members have extended notice of the meeting. Ensure they know what the meeting is about so they can prepare and assure their attendance. Prepare an agenda or list of discussion topics and inform members of the reports, investigations, and readings they need to do. Preparing the meeting place, security, food, etc., is also vital.
- **Conducting the Meeting:** Center immediately on the primary issue/agenda. Avoid dwelling too much on minor issues or matters that are not important. By focusing on important discussions, ensure the meeting finishes on time with fruitful results. Make sure there is equal participation from all members.

Avoid the monopoly of the few during discussion. Always summarize the flow of discussion so that everybody will know what level of the meeting has been achieved.

How does the committee continually improve its collective action?

To strengthen the committee's collective action, we need to:

- Cultivate and develop solidarity, mutual understanding, and sharing of work among the members. This will develop trust with each other, remove individualism, and help the collective leadership in performing its tasks.
- Develop a common language among the members through collective discussions, studies, and the continuous exchange of information. This will foster understanding and unity.
- Cultivate openness among members. Instead of hiding issues, we need to discuss problems or difficulties openly. We shouldn't wait for meetings to convey what we think or our problems or positions on important matters. Silence in meetings or in front of leadership will be counterproductive, while talking or criticizing outside of meetings can sow intrigue and disunity.
- Unite with our collective and learn to cooperate even if we are not comfortable with our comrades. Forming small groups, cliques, or a barkada system will weaken and decay the unity of the committee. We need to be helpful towards our comrades and guard against anything that will destroy the unity of the collective action of the committee.

(ARAK)

The committee's method of work

What is the importance of the committee's correct method of work?

It is not enough for the committee to just form decisions on how to do things. It needs to ensure that decisions are followed and implemented properly. Problems can arise even if proper decisions are made if we do not give importance to the correct manner of implementing these decisions.

There are already proven and established ways of committee work that can effectively lead the masses.

What does it mean that the secretary of the committee needs to excel and work like a "squad leader?"

We can compare the committee to a squad of a people's army, and the secretary to a "squad leader." To enable the secretary to effectively do their work, the committee must trust the secretary and support their efforts.

"Members of the squad" must learn to work and meet their responsibilities effectively.

To become an excellent "squad leader," one must be painstakingly diligent in their studies and deep in investigation. Leading a squad will be difficult without performing propaganda and organizing work for the "squad members," advancing their relationship with them, or studying how to conduct meetings appropriately.

It is extremely important to be understanding and supportive of one another, as well as maintaining strict honesty among the secretary and the members of the committee. This ensures unity in the movement of the "squad," which is the basis of effective leadership towards the masses.

What does "lay all problems out on the table" mean?
If any problem or difficulty arises, a meeting needs to be called immediately to "lay all problems out on the table" to discuss and derive competent decisions to solve the problem. If there is an existing problem and it is not "laid out on the table," it can hinder the facilitation of tasks and responsibilities. Failure to discuss and find solutions can impede the execution of duties and tasks.

This responsibility is not just the "squad leader's" but all members of the committee. Talking behind other people's backs won't help change the situation and can even add to the problem by causing confusion and making it worse.

What does "exchange of information" mean?

"Exchange of information" means that committee members must give reports to each other and exchange views on issues that catch their attention. This is important for advancing one common language.

Committee members must have a basic understanding of revolutionary theories and the National Democratic Revolutionary line. This ensures easy understanding and creates a unified view on issues that may arise while performing tasks.

Why is it important to be patient and to listen to the opinions and views of those at the lower levels and of the masses?

Comrades need excellent listening skills to hear the voices of those at the lower levels and of the masses. The decisions we make need to mirror these voices, ensuring that we are in alignment with the needs and perspectives of the broader community.

Will receive support from such decisions. In addition, they will feel that they are part of the decision-making process and we can show them how real democracy works.

We should not be ashamed to ask the opinion of those at the lower levels. We must not pretend to know what we do not know. This does not lessen our prestige; on the other hand, it increases it.

We also should not hastily agree or disagree on things that are being told to us at the lower levels. What they tell us will either be right or wrong and we need to analyze it properly. In addition, we need to be skillful in handling the clashing of ideas and to be able to patiently clarify in order that the correct thought will stand out. This way, we can form stronger unity between the leaders and members according to what is correct and what can help advance the revolution.

What does "learn to play the piano" mean?

We use ten fingers to play the piano. To make a good melody, these ten fingers don't just hit the keys but need to move with a clear pattern and coordination. It is not going to work if you use only some fingers while neglecting the others.

The committee does not face just one task, but a myriad of tasks. But just like playing the piano, the committee needs to have proper form and coordination to face these various tasks in order to effectively implement them. To do this, the committee needs to handle its main function at a given time. This is important, for the main function is the one that directs proper direction to smaller tasks. In addition, we need to clearly determine priorities at any given time to work on things that need to be done first.

Problems may arise while we are in the process of doing these tasks. We cannot just ignore this. We need to determine the primary problem at any given time and try to solve it. Solving the primary problem will give way to properly resolving other smaller problems.

This way, we can do our tasks smoothly, and we can say we excel in "playing the piano."

What does "hold tightly" to our primary tasks mean?

To "hold tightly" to our primary tasks means that we need to give our total attention and work to our primary tasks to ensure that we do them in proper time. We will fail in our work if we do not focus our attention on our primary tasks. Just like anything that we put in an open palm, it will only take a short time before it falls. We can also lose possession of anything if we hold it loosely in our hands.

No advancement will happen if we do not do our tasks and if we do not "hold" our tasks tightly.

What do we mean by "to excel in numbers?"

"Excelling in numbers" means that we need to give particular attention to the quantitative aspect of things or problems and make basic quantitative analysis. We can shape the quality of one's quantity, and there is no quality if there's no quantity.

We deal with the quantitative aspect of things in our daily tasks. If we do not "excel in numbers," we don't give attention to the quantitative aspect of these tasks, like statistics, primary percentages, and quantitative deadlines that give it quality. This can bring mistakes in our work.

For example, in our mass movement, we need to make proper investigations and analysis of the number of our active supporters, the neutral middle forces, and those who are our enemies. We must

not subjectively decide on the problem without concrete basis. This way, we can easily see the conditions of our tasks and make proper plans to advance their course.

What is the meaning of "give announcement to meetings?"

To "give announcement to meetings" means that we need to give timely warnings before we hold meetings. We also need to let those who can attend know what the meeting is about and what the things are that we will be discussing.

We also need to do proper preparation in making reports and drafting resolutions, the place of the meeting, and all logistics that go with it.

Meetings will not run smoothly, and time will be lost if we do not properly "give announcement to the meeting."

What does "fewer and better troops and simpler administration" mean?

It means that our sentences, speeches, articles, and resolutions must be made short and direct to the point. Meetings also need to be short and concise.

The key to this is proper preparation for the meeting so that we do not lose any valuable time and that the meeting will be more fruitful.

Why should we unite and cooperate with comrades who do not share our same ideas?

It is unavoidable that there will be differences in opinion within our ranks on matters that arise. This is because we come from different places and have different experiences. We must not only excel in uniting with comrades who share our opinion but also in uniting with those who have a variety of views.

This should also be our attitude toward comrades who make serious mistakes. We should not resent them and separate them from ourselves; we must prepare to unite with them in performing tasks.

Differences in opinion need to be resolved by conducting criticism and self-criticism. In resolving these differences, we need to always think of the interest of the revolution and of the broad masses, and not our self-interests. In conducting criticism and self-criticism, we need to start with a yearning to unite and advance what is right, elevating our unity to a higher level by sifting through the various ideas and finding what is accurate.

Why do we need to be guarded against arrogance?

We need to be guarded against arrogance, especially in leadership, to be able to maintain our principles and the unity in our ranks. Those who did not commit any mistakes and advance a lot of victories must not "become vain." It is important that we remain humble. We also need to be guarded against "lifting our own chair" and excessive praise of one's self in relation to the victories achieved. We need to maintain the principle of living simply and working hard.

Arrogance affects comrades who "become vain." Often, this comrade will have the tendency to become complacent, clumsy with decisions, and quick in doing their tasks, thinking they will not make mistakes. In meetings, they may think that they are always right and close their minds to listening and learning from others.

Why is it important to draw a line of difference on how we look at things?

This teaches us that we need to grasp the law of contradiction and look at different things as a whole, not just one-sidedly. This is important so that we can deeply look at and understand all things that surround us.

First and foremost, we need to draw a line.

Between the revolution and the counter-revolution, there are important issues to consider: for example, the issue of dictatorship.

Whenever we mention the word "dictatorship" during meetings, we immediately think of it as bad. We only view imperialism, big comprador bourgeois, and the landlord class as dictatorship, with the role of continuing the exploitation and oppression of the broad masses of society.

On the other hand, we say that we need to construct a democratic people's dictatorship—the dictatorship of the proletariat when we win the People's Democratic Revolution. This kind of dictatorship is different because it represents the interest of the masses against the ruling, oppressing class.

Second, inside the revolutionary ranks, we need to constantly differentiate right from wrong, between gains and shortcomings, and clarify which ones are primary and which are secondary.

For example, in assessing our actions, there will be a time when we point to mistakes and just center on them, failing to look at the bigger picture. On the other hand, if we only look at the positive things, we become blind to our weaknesses.

We can creatively and effectively handle our tasks if we look at their differences. To become experts in differentiating, we need to be resilient in our studies and deep in our analysis. We need to develop this kind of attitude.

www.ingramcontent.com/pod-product-compliance
Lightning Source LLC
LaVergne TN
LVHW022057200926
848481LV00003B/949
* 9 7 9 8 3 4 9 5 4 7 3 4 8 *